I AM POWERFUL

*How to Create Abundance
in All Areas of Your Life*

Eleni Giakatis

I AM POWERFUL: How to Create Abundance in All Areas of Your Life
www.elenigiakatis.com
Copyright © 2023 Eleni Giakatis

Paperback ISBN: 979-8-3677-8875-4

All rights reserved. No portion of this book may be reproduced mechanically, electronically, or by any other means, including photocopying, without permission of the publisher or author except in the case of brief quotations embodied in critical articles and reviews. It is illegal to copy this book, post it to a website, or distribute it by any other means without permission from the publisher or author.

References to internet websites (URLs) were accurate at the time of writing. Authors and the publishers are not responsible for URLs that may have expired or changed since the manuscript was prepared.

Limits of Liability and Disclaimer of Warranty
The author and publisher shall not be liable for your misuse of the enclosed material. This book is strictly for informational and educational purposes only.

Warning – Disclaimer
The purpose of this book is to educate and entertain. The author and/or publisher do not guarantee that anyone following these techniques, suggestions, tips, ideas, or strategies will become successful. The author and/or publisher shall have neither liability nor responsibility to anyone with respect to any loss or damage caused, or alleged to be caused, directly or indirectly by the information contained in this book.

Publisher
10-10-10 Publishing
Markham, ON Canada

Printed in Canada and the United States of America

*I would like to dedicate this book to my sister,
Christena Alyssandratos. You are my rock,
my pillar of strength and my "go-to" person.
You are a beautiful, gentle and caring soul.*

*I am so grateful that as each year passes,
our connection and bond only grows stronger.*

*Thank you for always being there to celebrate
wins and listen to my struggles. I truly appreciate everything
you do for me and my family. I can't wait
to watch you flourish as a life coach, and I know you
will be remarkable at helping those around you!*

Table of Contents

From Shades of Grey to Technicolor..xi
Acknowledgements xiii
Foreword..xix
Introduction..xxi

Chapter 1: I Am Blissful 1
The Power is Within You 3
The Power of "I AM" 4
I AM Affirmations 7
Manage Your Triggers..8
Change Your Thoughts, Change Your Behaviors 10
The Importance of Mindfulness 14
Chapter 1 Takeaways 16

Chapter 2: I Am Glowing 19
I AM Radiant 22
Visualization 23
The Necessary Steps for Visualization...26
Be Willing to Accept Your Gifts 27
The Power of Your Body 28
A Glowing Body 29
Healthy Eating..30
Weight Scales 33
Exercise..33
Yoga Practice...39
Sleep 35
Feeling & Looking Magnificent! 37
Chapter 2 Takeaways 39

Chapter 3: I Am Smitten 41
Importance of Your Romantic Relationships 44
Self-Worth and Self-Esteem 46
Acting as if It Has Already Occurred 48
Soulmates 49
Kindred Spirits 51
Twin Flames 52
Karmic Relationships 53
Expectations 54
Establishing Healthy Boundaries 55
Negative People 57
Intimacy 58
The Five Love Languages 59
Attraction 60
Chapter 3 Takeaways 63

Chapter 4: I Am A Bombshell 65
Improve Your Character, Raise Your Vibration 68
How Confident Are You? 69
Train Your Mind to Think Positive 70
The Power of Self-Talk 71
Increased Endorphins: Feelings of Happiness 73
Connect with Loved Ones 74
Surround Yourself with Joyful Things 75
Feed Yourself Positivity... Through Your Belly! 76
Other Ways to Increase Your Vibration 77
Chapter 4 Takeaways 78

Chapter 5: I Am Fearless ... 81
Facing Your Fear ... 84
Fear of Public Speaking ... 85
Fear of Heights ... 86
Fear of Failure ... 87
Fear of Aging ... 89
Overcoming Your Fear ... 90
Act "As If" ... 92
Meditation for Eradicating Fears ... 93
Chapter 5 Takeaways ... 96

Chapter 6: I Am the Creator of My Destiny ... 97
The Magic Happens in the Present Moment ... 100
The Secret Ingredient! ... 100
What is the Law of Attraction? ... 101
Recognizing a Blessing in Disguise ... 104
The Art of Surrender ... 105
The Process of the Law of Attraction ... 107
You Are the Creator of Your Destiny ... 110
Other Important Universal Laws ... 111
The Law of Relativity ... 111
The Law of Cause and Effect ... 112
The Law of Polarity ... 112
The Law of Gestation ... 112
The Law of Rhythm ... 113
The Law of Transmutation ... 113
Chapter 6 Takeaways ... 114

Chapter 7: I Am a Money Magnet 115
Give and You Shall Receive 119
Mental Conflict..120
Abundant Mindset — Very Important! 123
Blocks to Wealth 126
Allow Money to Flow In...128
Chapter 7 Takeaways 130

Chapter 8: I Am Successful 133
How to Be Successful 136
Are You Living Your Life Purpose? 137
Create the Space: Train Your Mind to Think Positively............144
Give Back 145
Ho'oponopono Method 147
The Four Basic Steps of Ho'oponopono 148
Chapter 8 Takeaways 151

Chapter 9: I Am a Business Guru..153
Customer Service 155
Communication Styles & Creating Relationships......................158
Body Language 160
Create a Financial Plan..161
How Does a Great Leader Operate? 164
Lead with Kindness...165
Chapter 9 Takeaways 166

Chapter 10: I Am the Pilot 167
Managing Change..169
The Truth 170
Your Ship Has Arrived 172
Maintaining a Positive Attitude...173
The Universe is on Your Side! 174
Creation 101 176

From Shades of Grey to Technicolor

Here I AM.
In the stillness of the day
I ponder the meaning of life

Redirecting my mindset
Out of the fabricated faux pas existence

Every single minute of the day
Needs to be treasured

Why do we behave like robots?
Wilting our sacred time on this earth
Carelessly away….

Allowing youth and vitality to escape us
So thoughtlessly

Buying into the illusion of stress and fear
Accepting as fact that we cannot escape
Our perceived reality

When there has always been a lighted route
All that's required is a switch from off to on
A mindful decision to change course
No longer accepting status quo

For bonuses go to www.elenigiakatis.com

Picking ourselves up with love and compassion
Turning towards the brightly lit road
Change the course of our earthly journey
Towards enlightenment, love and bliss

Shedding the grey existence
Welcoming the rainbow, cheerful life
That was always there

We were lost
Now, we have found our way
Home.

~ Eleni Giakatis

Acknowledgements

I would like to thank my dear immediate family, **Tom, Billy and Destiny,** for all your support and love. You give me strength and inspiration to level up in the world. Thank you for cheering me on and believing in me. You are my pillars of strength and I know you always have my back. I am grateful for your encouragement and for always helping me celebrate all my accomplishments. I love you with all my heart and soul forever!

Thank you to other members of my family: my parents **Katina, George and Magdelina;** my son-in-law **Paul** and beautiful granddaughter **Skyler Eleni Christina;** my future daughter-in-law, **Marika;** my sister **Christena,** brother-in-law **Nick,** nieces **Katie and Angelica;** my nieces **Patty and Mary** and their beautiful families and brother-in-law **Pando;** my godchild **Evelyn,** and brother-in-law **Phill.** You are my tight circle of love and light.

I would like to thank my beloved sister, **Alexia,** who passed away in March 2022 after courageously fighting ovarian cancer for 10 years. Her strength was like nothing I have ever seen, and her desire to live was paramount. She persevered and continuously recovered after so many years of various cancer treatments. (The pain this epic woman suffered was beyond reason.) She had so much love and vitality for life, and such a sense of humour! I thank her for the strength and courage you taught me and for her fearless perseverance for life until her last breath.

For bonuses go to ...

I would like to thank my niece, **Constance (Connie).** You are an extraordinary young lady who has surpassed many challenges in your life, including a health-related issue. You are a true example of strength, kindness and compassion. You were a daughter extraordinaire during your mother's (my sister Alexia's) fight with cancer and took on the leadership role in your mother's healthcare regime with such grace. During this difficult time, you also fought your own battle with cancer, and I am grateful you are now healthy and strong and ready to live out your dreams. I am always here for you.

Thank you to my angels in heaven: my mother-in-law **Maria** and my sister-in-law **Sandra.** You were gentle women whose entire lives revolved around family. You meant the world to me, and I am forever grateful for your love and support. Thank you for the integral role you played in my life by offering me and my children unconditional love.

Thank you to my friend **Dragana.** You are a loving, authentic, intuitive and all-around amazing friend. I am always grateful for our daily touch-ins as they make me feel seen and supported. I am so proud of your strength and leadership skills and how, through many challenges, you have persevered and overcome all obstacles. I am so proud that you continue to uplevel your life and enhance the lives of those around you.

Thank you, **Doctor Victoria** (hypnotherapist), for your expertise, advice and very powerful ability to delete negative emotions and replace them with tools for a happier and more fulfilling life. You empower people to live peaceful and joyous lives. I am always learning something new from you.

Thanks to my friend **Hannah,** for all your support, love and inspiring conversations. You were integral in getting me to come out of my shell in my earlier years. Thanks for encouraging me to be fearless, execute my passions in life, and let my hair down.

Thank you, **Josey,** for your genuine support and friendship. You are a strong person and have overcome enormous challenges in your life. Thanks for encouraging me to be my best and to live a fearless life of fun and adventure.

Thank you, **Philip S,** for your collaboration and friendship over the past several years. You have an exceptional sense of humor, which is very fun, and your high energy is contagious. I appreciate all your support and collaboration.

I would like to thank **Andru,** my current VP. You are next level! God has a special place for people like you, and I am glad to be given the opportunity to get to know you better. Thank you so much for all your kind support during difficult times in my life. I really appreciate it. You encouraged me to shine, which subsequently led me to win the top award in the bank in 2022. Thank you so much!

I would like to thank **Rick,** my previous VP. I appreciated your support and leadership. You always led with kindness and compassion and encouraged me to be innovative and think outside the box. Thank you for supporting all my personal development strategies. I truly appreciate it!

Thank you, **Marta,** of Serene Med Spa Salon. You are an exceptional entrepreneur who truly cares about her clients. Your services are extraordinary!

For bonuses go to ...

My friend **Denny,** thank you for your insights, support and friendship. During COVID, I really enjoyed our group neighborhood power walks and inspirational chats. You're an amazing person.

Rosetta, you have been an exquisite friend for many years. I am grateful I had a chance to learn so much about banking from you when I first started my career. Sharing your expertise and wealth of knowledge over the years was greatly appreciated. You were an awesome mentor and added value to people's lives.

To my family in Greece: Thank you to my cousin **Eleni.** We hadn't seen each other for many years, but when we met, it was like we had known each other forever. Thank you for your hospitality. We had such an exceptional time when we visited. Thank you to **Filippos, Giannis and Fania.** Also, my special aunt, **Thea Fota.** She's the classiest woman I have ever met. When she came to Canada, oh my goodness, she bought that red faux fur coat. She was a Diva. She's a phenomenal woman. I wish I could have spent my childhood years within her guidance. I'm sure my leadership skills would have escalated exponentially! Thanks also to **Theo Kiryiako,** such an amazing and kind person, and my cousin **Niko.** Also, my cousins in Greece, **Nikoletta, Chris and family. Voula and family** and **Valentina and her beautiful son**. My deceased **Yiayia Para** was also a big part of my life. I loved her dearly. May she RIP.

Thank you, **Zoe,** for your support, encouragement and candid chats. You offered caring advice and recommendations. Thank you for being there for me and my family over the years especially during the challenging times.

www.elenigiakatis.com

I want to thank **Natalie** and **Liz** on Raymond Aaron's team for supporting me through this awesome experience of writing my book. I appreciate all your support and guidance.

Foreword

When you wake up in the morning do you feel a sense of hope and purpose? Or do you feel run down and generally uninspired?

When you think about all the aspects of your life, are you full of vigor and joy? Or again, are you feeling down, and simply slogging away at the "every day"?

A life of abundance is waiting for you, and Eleni is a go-to expert on how to live your best life, whether it be in work or play. Eleni clearly lays out how you can access the abundance that is your birthright, via every single pathway in your life. You are a unique individual living a unique life. Reaching your most passionate goals starts with your mindset, and Eleni is here to give you all the tools you need to do that … whether it be bringing something specific into your life or just feeling more young and vibrant, or even attracting a romantic partnership. The pages of this valuable book are bursting with resources.

With over 25+ years in the financial corporate world, Eleni has not only seen the inside workings of big business, but has also been a leader. She has taken great pride in cultivating deep and personal relationships, and being able to get to the heart of the matter, whether it be in or out of the office. Through her own trials and tribulations, she has persevered in both her career and her personal life. Always looked to as someone with a deep

For bonuses go to www.elenigiakatis.com

knowledge of how to live a life of abundance, Eleni is now ready to share this wisdom with YOU.

I hope you stay open and hopeful to all the possibilities this life may offer you. Eleni is here to help you claim the abundance you deserve.

Raymond Aaron
New York Times **Bestselling Author**

Introduction

When you dream about your ideal life, do you feel empowered and ready to go? Or do you feel confused or overwhelmed? No matter where you are starting from, be it from creating new dreams and possibilities seemingly out of nothing, or if you want to create something even bigger and better than what is in your life already, I welcome you to this journey!

I have written this book for YOU! This book is so much more than just improving your life. It is about connecting to a deep power that exists within. Right now, as you are reading this, the possibility of creating a happy and fulfilling life is within your reach. No matter your circumstance today, you have the power to create deep and profound change in all areas of your life: health, relationships, career and finances.

Much of the knowledge and practices that I will be sharing have been part of my life for the last 20 years. Time after time, I have been approached by people that I know (and even strangers!), to share what my best practices are and how I create and attract all that I am blessed to have in my life. From skin care to aging elegantly, climbing the corporate ladder with success, to feeling positive and enjoying abundant amounts of energy, I have so many possibilities to share with you. I can confidently say that I have also certainly mastered the pendulum momentum of balancing a career and family life as well (at times, the hardest one to manage!) It is time that I open up my circle beyond people that I coach and mentor, to YOU, and ensure you not only understand but BELIEVE you have the POWER to cultivate a truly magnificent life.

It all starts with the phrase "I AM." When these two words are placed together and declared through your lips or written onto paper, miracles can happen. This phrase is deeply sacred and represents that which is bigger than you; be it God, Source energy, the Universe…whatever you wish to name it. When you say, "I AM," you connect to this energy, and this is where and when great changes can happen in your life. You transcend your own limitations and invite in possibilities.

There is a bit of everything in this book. We will dive into health, finances, career, love life and generally being the BOSS of your life. Chapter by chapter, I will build you up to realize your greatest potential. No doubt this will be one of those books that you go back to again and again as you keep leveling UP!

If I have helped even ONE person feel better about themselves and their life, I will have achieved my goal and purpose in writing this book. I want to guide you through not only the process of creating your life, but also establishing a deep sense of pride in yourself for doing the work and making it happen! If you are here, you are ready for the changes that await you…

Chapter 1

I AM BLISSFUL:
Happiness and Getting in Tune
with Your Higher Self

*"There isn't anything that
I cannot be or do or have."*
– Abraham Hicks

When you wake up first thing in the morning and start your day, how do you feel? This is of course after shaking out the cobwebs of your sleep and having a great cup of coffee or tea!-When you begin to go through the motions of your day, do you have a sense of ease and joy, or do you have a case of the doldrums and just don't seem to care? If it's the latter, then I am glad you are here!

The purpose of your life is to be happy! Happiness is that inherent sense of bliss and an uplifting feeling that comes from within yourself. It is not something you will ever find outside of yourself, no matter how hard you try. No amount of shopping, dining out, vacations or distractions will truly make you authentically happy. It is an inside job.

The Power is Within You

One thing you must come to understand right away is that we are spiritual beings living a human experience. Let me say that one more time: YOU are a spiritual being living a human experience. What does this mean? One way to look at it is that you are more than your body and experiences. The purest essence of yourself is your soul or higher self. It operates differently than your body or the material world that surrounds you.

For bonuses go to ...

Getting to know this part of you is how you are going to access authentic happiness and joy in your life. It is important to understand that your higher self works directly with your mind. This has nothing to do with your ego. Your ego is your need to be right—self-esteem or a sense of self-importance—and it all feeds into your sense of personal reality.

Your ego enjoys center stage and wants to run your life. If your view of yourself is negative, then you will have negative thoughts about yourself, which can lead to negative situations that can cause unhappy experiences in your life.

It has everything to do with your inner voice and connecting to your instincts. It may take a lot of practice, especially depending on how connected to your inner voice you are right now. But believe me, once you connect with the inherent wisdom that is inside your body, a world of possibilities will open up for you. This is where you can harness the power of **"I AM."**

The Power of "I AM"

Everything you think and say is important. Every word you share with yourself or others has significant power in your life. When we say the specific words **"I AM,"** we are directly connecting with a power that is bigger than us. No matter what you want to call it—Source energy, God, higher self, Universe—this is what created you and everything around you. When you say, "I AM," and actively visualize what you are trying to align yourself with, you are creating a direct connection to this powerful energy!

"I AM" can create miracles! This phrase can help you create a life of abundance and cultivate so much love in your life, you won't even know what to do with it all! However, be mindful and cautious as it can also create catastrophe and bring negativity into your world. This can happen when you use the phrase in a negative manner. It will attract that negativity into your life. The problem with negative thoughts is that they can become self-fulfilling prophecies. If we use the power of I AM in a negative manner, we can talk ourselves into believing that we're not good enough, and this will result in a negative impact in our personal lives, our relationships and our careers.

Sometimes people say, "I'm not lucky." This could refer to finding a parking spot close to their location. This becomes a self-fulfilling prophecy because they never will. I, on the other hand, ALWAYS find a parking spot easily and effortlessly right up front. It's a given now; I always find a free parking spot up front—it never fails. Even in a busy mall where the parking lot is full, someone will depart just as I pull up and free up the space for me. This did not happen overnight for me. (Although it absolutely could!) Once I got the hang of it, I decided to branch out. I started to create easy left turns when I'm driving my car. I just declare that there will be no cars to hinder my left turn. It works like a charm!

Never forget that the words you use in your thoughts will create feelings, and these feelings will affect your physical world. I'm certain that if you were to take some time and reflect on your own relationship to words, you may see (and feel!) the correlation.

When I first became a bank manager several years ago, I was sitting at a regional bank conference listening to a presentation conducted by the CEO of the financial institution that I worked for. I was in a room with 200 other dynamic bank managers in my region, and I remember feeling gratitude, sheer bliss and a sense of joy to be in a room filled with these experienced

For bonuses go to ...

professionals that I admired. The CEO of the company was presenting the four main areas of focus for the year. There was a new objective that year and, in an effort to create excitement and successful results, he stated that there would be an award for the top bank manager in the region on a quarterly basis. Each quarter, the recipient would receive an all-inclusive weekend getaway for two, to various places in the world, with all expenses paid and spending money included. I had decided at that moment in my state of joy that I was going to WIN ALL FOUR PRIZES for the year. I had such a strong and loving feeling in my gut that I could do this. I obviously didn't know how this was going to occur but I set a very powerful intention that I felt throughout my body, when I affirmed to myself that **"I AM winning all awards."**

What happened next was extremely magical! To my surprise and delight, I fulfilled my prophecy! Keep in mind that this was a brand-new job and I had no idea how I would accomplish this, but everything just clicked. This is the power of the Universe at play.

My husband and I went on to enjoy getaways in downtown Toronto, Niagara Falls (Canada), New York City and Arizona. That was a very successful year for me. On top of being awarded the trips, I was constantly recognized and even received a promotion the following year.

When you learn how to harness the power of "I AM," you will develop a deep inner wisdom and have the strength to change your life. Your life will change as you begin to make good decisions and exercise better judgment as to what will positively or negatively impact your life.

I AM Affirmations

You can leverage the power of **I AM** in daily affirmations. These are positive statements that can help you challenge and overcome self-sabotaging and negative thoughts. When you repeat them often, and **believe in them**, you can start to make positive changes. It is important to shift your mindset in a positive manner when saying affirmations. Get your whole self-involved and say them from the heart with love and conviction. Affirmations are not successful if you can't switch out of a negative emotion into a positive one by saying them. For example, if you feel angry and say, "I AM peaceful," it won't work! YOU have to *feel* yourself out of anger. As you begin, it can help to take a few deep breaths, close your eyes and get into it. Even during tough times in your life when you are struggling, step up your "I AM" affirmations and always commit to feel the love in your heart. Affirmations are best said with conviction and out loud.

Examples of positive affirmations that can be used regularly throughout the day are:

- *I AM happy.*
- *I AM loveable.*
- *I AM magnificent.*
- *I AM intelligent.*
- *I AM successful.*
- *I AM a money magnet.*
- *I AM healthy.*
- *I AM unstoppable.*
- *I AM enough.*
- *I AM worthy.*
- *I AM beautiful.*
- *I AM a winner.*

For bonuses go to ...

Throughout the book, we will continue to explore how, through affirmations, you can become your most powerful self.

Manage Your Triggers

I bet if you sit down right now with a cup of coffee or tea, you would be able to pinpoint some things in your life that make you feel annoyed, frustrated or even angry. Sure, this could be simple pet peeves, but I am also talking about the things that you encounter in your life repeatedly that can bring you into a more negative state of mind. It's important to begin recognizing these triggers; the things that can take you from a positive to a negative state of mind in a flash.

It is imperative that you start getting to know when you feel triggered into negative emotions. I am sure that when you start paying attention, you will understand that this most likely happens daily, if not several times a day! When you feel triggered into negative emotions, learning to reset yourself back into a more positive state of "I AM" is a lifesaver and will become one of the most powerful ways you can, in a sense, be your own ally. I'd love to share with you a snapshot of what this has looked like for me in the past, to give you a sense of what I am talking about.

When I first started working as a bank manager for a major financial institution in Canada, I remember waking up every day full of positive energy and inspiration. I felt I could take on anything that the day would throw at me, no matter how big or small. But of course, I would encounter numerous challenges throughout my day that would trigger my negative energy and bring me down. Sometimes it was an irate client that I needed to manage, or a disgruntled employee that needed assistance.

Things involving conflict or other people bringing their negative energy into my workspace, could easily drain my energy. It's difficult to maintain a positive façade if you're constantly challenged. My customer service standard was that our bank would never have a bad day. I prided myself in ensuring we provided exceptional customer service to our clients. I had to lead by example to my team. I felt especially responsible as I was a leader in my company. I wanted to show up for my team and my clients as my best self and represent the company as a whole, in a good light. How can you do that if you are constantly being dragged down, down, down into a negative state of being?

I realized that many things were manageable and it was up to me to change the energy I felt, from negative to positive. I began applying some simple tactics that I could use throughout my day. One of my favorite ways was simply getting into my car and going for a drive to get a coffee. The change of scenery helped me clear my head and reset my mindset to one that was more of a calm and pleasant state of being. WOW. I cannot begin to tell you how that simple tactic really saved me some days! Get up and MOVE away from the challenge space and go get some fresh air! This tactic is extremely effective, especially if you're with another person or a group of people that cannot come to a consensus. Take a break and leave the room. When you all reunite after the break, you'll have a less stringent energy that you can work with to come to an agreement.

It doesn't matter if you are a CEO, general worker, stay at home parent or student… Anyone will benefit by taking some time and learning about what tactics you can employ to bring yourself back into a positive frame of mind. As you go about your day-to-day, there is no doubt you will get triggered emotionally. However, you can decide to make the necessary changes and not

For bonuses go to ...

stay in a negative state. You want to start the day in "I AM Blissful" and try to stay there as best you can until your head hits the pillow at the end of the night. It takes a lot of practice!

The important thing to remember is that you must do something to change your negative mindset to one of peace. What works for you? It doesn't have to be anything fancy! Try my tactic of going to get a coffee. How much simpler can it be?

Here are some additional ideas to ignite your own inspiration:

- Leave whatever you are doing, walk away to a quieter space and take 5 deep, conscious breaths, in through your nose and out through your mouth.
- Do some simple stretches.
- Listen to your favorite uplifting song.
- Go outside for a walk around the block to clear your head.
- Go for a walk in the park and surround yourself in nature. Eat your lunch in the park if this is an option.
- Call a close friend/family member and look for support, or just have a chat to get out of your headspace.

It takes practice, especially if this is a new way of operating, and that's okay! Be easy on yourself and recognize that you are doing the important work of changing your state of being by changing your mind and reactions. Find what really works for you and you will soon see and FEEL these changes. You will keep yourself aligned with more positive states of being.

Change Your Thoughts, Change Your Behaviors

What is becoming very clear here is that how you **THINK**, **ACT** and **FEEL** will directly reflect your reality. In other words, the only way to create change is to embrace and apply it in your life. Creating new habits will create a new mindset and will help you feel different emotions.

If 90% of your thoughts are the same, then it stands to reason that you will make the same choices 90% of the time. It's imperative to break your own thought cycles in order to change. There are a few ways to begin doing this immediately.

First, you must decide that you no longer wish to act the same way! Make an agreement within yourself that you **want** to change. This is CRITICAL. Think about it—how are you going to dive into creating change when you haven't made that agreement within yourself? I know it may sound silly; but really, this is where it starts. You must be crystal clear and very honest with yourself that you are ready for change. This can be one of the most exciting and rewarding steps! When you come to realize that you are ready and willing to create change, anything is possible!

It is about interrupting your current state of being. It will require you to make new choices consistently on a day-to-day basis. Guess what? It is going to feel uncomfortable and, of course, it should. I almost think that if it isn't uncomfortable, then you really aren't being honest and trying. You will be tested, and you will be challenged. But never forget, this space of uncertainty is where the MAGIC happens.

You interrupt your state of being with your thoughts. You must choose new thoughts to begin playing out new behaviors. Sometimes we need a little help to recognize our negative thought patterns. Maybe wearing something specific on yourself, like a ring or bracelet, can be a helpful reminder of a new thought pattern that you are trying to cultivate. For example, I had a client that had a bracelet on her wrist that whenever she saw it, she would say to herself, "I AM Worthy," to combat her constant negative thought patterns of thinking that she was not good enough in many areas of her life. The behavior that emerged was of more confidence and less second guessing. You can make it personal and meaningful to you.

Feeling your negative emotions is just as important as feeling your positive ones. For example, if you feel sad, feel your sadness fully. Then ask yourself WHY you are feeling this way? What is really going on? It's interesting to note that when you welcome a negative emotion, it dissipates very quickly. It also loses potency and eventually disappears! The invitation to feel is a loving gesture. When you experience feelings of love and compassion toward yourself, it trumps negative feelings. Really take this in… When you deliberately realize you're thinking negative thoughts, you CAN press "reset"—this is HUGE! If you can take it one step forward and pivot by feeling love and compassion within your heart, you're building up some serious ammunition for positive change.

Another inspiring way to begin to change behaviors is to begin to *feel* as if you are already playing out your new patterns of behavior. Cultivating specific emotions can send new signals to your brain and actually begin the process of changing your behaviors without actual action, but simply through feeling. For example, if you wanted to be healthier, you would make a conscious decision to stop eating ice cream after dinner. A good starting point would be to remove ice cream or other unhealthy snacks from your home and align with your new self-image. Start feeling powerful that you are sticking to your plan!

If you are able to feel as if you are already living your new behaviors and leading your life with your new thought patterns in place, you will be unstoppable and able to put your mind to anything you choose. Just watch as your thoughts and emotions translate to your physical experience. The urges will subside and, soon enough, that habit will vanish. You will then emerge as your new gorgeous, healthy self, feeling magnificent.

Empower yourself by deprogramming the old and creating the new. One way to start is just to simply pick one behavior that you wish to delete immediately. Can you pinpoint something you do habitually that is not in line with who you wish to be? Perhaps it is putting off your daily walk, or not quite drinking enough water during the day. Get to work on focusing on that one thing… Recognize what thought occurs before you engage in it. This is where the power is—it is here that you want to work on disintegrating it. When this thought pops up in your mind, work on releasing it or even pressing delete like you would on a keyboard. Commit to doing this repeatedly… Fill the newfound space in your thoughts with COURAGE! Perhaps state a powerful affirmation like I AM UNSTOPPABLE! You are committing to being uncomfortable with the process of change. ALWAYS give yourself credit for executing this new way of living, and recognize that you are doing this for yourself and that you have your own back. *Feeling* differently will bring forth new experiences in your life and an abundant mindset. This will translate into exceptional results, no matter what you are working on. When you work on deep rooted change within your psyche, massive changes will appear in your life.

Never forget: Your brain is the most powerful tool that you can't buy and no one can take from you. The more you train your mind and manage your thoughts, the more successful your results will be.

For bonuses go to ...

The Importance of Mindfulness

When it comes down to it, the practice of mindfulness will be your biggest support when making changes and bringing yourself to more "I AM" moments. Through mindfulness, you will be able to remain present and continue to access your intuition, which is your higher self, and guess what? Your higher self always has the right answer for the moment. Mindfulness is the ability to bring yourself into the present moment. One way that I love, and feel is very potent, is through the practice of gratitude. Giving thanks and counting your blessings will always keep you in touch with the energy of love. Love is the highest vibration of positive energy that you can experience, so why not do everything possible to access this plane of existence? Gratitude is a direct path to a more blissful experience.

One of the other most powerful tools of mindfulness is meditation. Meditation is essential in helping to settle your ego in order to let your higher consciousness come forth. If you are not convinced, remember that your thoughts directly impact your energy. This is what meditation is all about: creating a relationship with your thoughts.

Meditation helps to improve focus, manage your stress levels and provides an overall sense of calmness and peace of mind. Learning how to meditate is straightforward and the benefits can come quickly. Ensure you set aside time for your meditation practice; even just a few minutes a day can make a big difference in your life. Find a comfortable spot and get ready to relax.

In my daily meditation routine, I have a favorite chair that I sit on every morning. I bring my coffee with me and sip on it as I glance outside in nature. I drink my coffee and close my eyes as

I enter the silence. I start to relax my body slowly from the top of my head to the bottom of my feet. I relax all muscles until my body feels light. Sometimes I play a guided 15-minute meditation, especially if there's a lot going on and I have difficulty controlling my thoughts. A guided meditation helps because I follow the instructions and quiet my thoughts easily. Other times, I can get into the silence and calm my mind and "let go" on my own. I simply surrender.

The purpose of mindful meditation is to become more present and open hearted to everything you do during your day. Stillness allows you to obtain answers to your issues or questions from the Universe. At the beginning, your thoughts will wander and you may have trouble emptying your mind, which is perfectly normal.

I recommend starting with a simple and short, guided meditation practice to help you connect and get comfortable observing your thoughts. There are many available at the click of a button online. Start with five minutes a day and gradually work your way up to longer periods of time, eventually landing on something a bit longer that feels like it serves you. (I personally practice 15 minutes a day, but each person is different!) If you feel you don't have 15 minutes per day to meditate, then you definitely need to meditate for at least an hour!

Make maintaining a high vibration a priority in your life. Recognize when your mind begins dwindling and reverting back to old thought patterns and old behaviors. Trust in the work that you do to change this. Trust in yourself and be willing to surrender completely to the work and the outcome. When in doubt, commit to staying neutral (which can feel like being mindful) until you understand the next step to feeling positive and back on your path of being empowered. Remember: You are not a victim in your life, and you possess the power to take responsibility for your life. Stop blaming others and take action. And when in doubt, ask for help! Seek a mentor or hire a coach to work with. We can all use some help sometimes. Remember to revert to gratitude and leverage I AM statements, such as I AM happy and grateful that I AM healthy and prosperous!

Let's continue to examine the powerful realms of "I AM" and how it can directly impact every aspect of your life. Examining your relationship to your physical body comes next. It can quickly determine your success as your mind and body are deeply interconnected. The next chapter will offer some great insights on how you can use your mind to affect your body and uplevel your relationship with yourself.

Chapter 1 Takeaways:

- Happiness is an inside job!

- When you speak the statement "I AM," you are connecting into the bigger energies of the Universe.

- When you begin using and believing in **positive affirmations** daily, you will see change in your life.

- Learning how to recognize and **manage triggers** that take you to a negative thought, will keep you aligned with positive energy.

- How you **THINK, ACT and FEEL** all need to be aligned to create change (you cannot change one without the other).

- **Meditation** practice is essential to cultivate in order to settle your ego and keep you connected to a flow state.

- Make maintaining a high vibration a priority in your life.

Chapter 2

I AM GLOWING:
Harnessing the Power of Your Physical Body

> *"Beauty begins the moment
> you decide to be yourself."*
> **– Coco Chanel**

Are you as excited as I am to be here? Trust me when I say that it is not an accident that you have this book in your hand. I am so grateful that you are here as we begin to unpack layer after layer of this powerful glowing connection to your mind and body!

We laid the foundation of the work in the first chapter by delving in and coming to understand that your words hold way more power than you ever imagined. Now the second layer is to connect to your physical body. This isn't just about how to feel good and look good, but it will be about cultivating a deep sense of self-care and self-love! When you are out making your way in this crazy and wild world of ours, self-love is your biggest secret weapon. Learning how to love yourself EXACTLY as you are right now—unconditionally—will change your life.

Think of it as getting your body ready to work with all the power that you are bringing into your life. If you are not feeling good in your body, it doesn't matter how many mantras you try to work with or how many times you try to attract things toward you; you will not be ready to harness any higher energy effectively.

On the days I take a little extra time to get ready, put some lipstick on and wear a cute outfit and shoes, I walk into the world feeling like a million dollars! It really starts from my mindset. I feel magnificent inside and am glowing on the outside. I smile more and it entices people to smile back.

> *"Every time you smile at someone, it is an action of love, a gift to that person, a beautiful thing."*
> – Mother Teresa

Let's examine the mind/body connection and how you can connect to yourself in a healthy, positive and sustainable way. Yes, of course, we will touch upon the importance of exercise and making healthy nutritional choices, but it is more than that. I want you to be able to cultivate powerful feelings of self-love and self-worth and wake up in the morning always believing that you deserve the best, and then have the energy to work for it as well. I want you to wake up and know deep down inside that YOU ARE ENOUGH. So, grab a nice cup of coffee, herbal tea or some water with lemon and let's do this!

I AM Radiant

Look at you, sitting there and glowing. Yes, I am talking to YOU… How did it make you feel when I said that? Are you able to take a compliment? Are you able to sit in your body and feel worthy… feel like you are enough?

This is something you must connect with to really open yourself up to possibilities. And yes, it can be difficult! Feelings of unworthiness are learned when we are young and can stay with us into adulthood. When we are babies, we possess an innate sense of great courage and joy. This helped us to learn new things every day, and we understood how to become more and more independent. We were willing to take risks because we could feel that sense of joy when we figured something out, and we were able to level up in our development. But as we got older, it seems we lost this willingness to take a risk. It makes sense though. Now, as an adult, when it comes down to it, all you have is yourself to rely on, so you want to stay safe and comfortable. You may feel that staying at your baseline is really all you are WORTH. Well, I am here to tell you, that is NOT TRUE. As you sit there reading this book, you have the potential to step into your power. You must believe me when I say that you were born ready and worthy to live an incredible life—no matter where you are starting from, you are ENOUGH.

Let's set the foundation for your transformation, shall we? First things first, stop criticizing yourself. Easier said than done, right? I am sure there are things that you tend to dislike, specifically like criticizing your body. We have all been guilty of this at one time or another. There are those aspects of your body you may not be happy with or love. Well, I must tell you, this is no way to operate, especially when setting yourself up to live a powerful life. Your body is a miracle, and it's the only one you have. It deserves the utmost respect, admiration and love. When you criticize your own body, you don't promote positive energy to come into your life. When you take care of your body and engage in a healthy lifestyle, you'll find your respect for your body will increase, and that nasty voice inside your head will be shushed.

It is all about changing your negative mindset to a positive one. This keeps good energy flowing into your life, no matter what you are focusing on. An incredible tool to use is visualization.

Visualization

First, you can utilize visualization to bring you back into a positive mindset on the spot. You know how people talk about going to their "happy place?" Well, I wholeheartedly recommend it! When you can take yourself somewhere in your mind, where you can experience joy and relaxation, it can bring those feelings into your body no matter where you are. My happy place is the beach (I love the beach). When I am feeling stressed or I need a positive boost, I'll bring up a pic from a past vacation and let myself deeply remember the time spent there: the hot sun on my skin, relaxing in a comfortable chair with a refreshing drink in hand, hearing the ancient ocean tides dancing on the shore... I felt radiant in that moment on the beach, and it makes me feel radiant in the present moment as well! What is your happy place? Where can you let your mind go so that you can feel alive, positive and radiant?

Visualization helps you keep your mind focused on empowering yourself. Feel free to use all pertinent senses when embarking on a powerful visualization of what you wish to manifest. The more colors you visualize, the more various sounds you hear, the more touch and feeling sensations you can imagine, the better! I decided to give this a try in a playful manner. I chose to visualize a red rose. I saw it in my mind and could smell the sweet aroma. I imagined I could feel the soft petals. I pictured the beautiful, rich color of a red rose. I then decided to visualize many red roses and I felt delighted and happy. I connected with this joyous feeling within my heart, and I claimed these roses as my own. I set a powerful intention that these roses would be mine in Divine time. Then I simply let it go and actually forgot about it. I set the intention and let it go because I TRUST and BELIEVE that the Universe will deliver it to me. To my sheer amazement, that weekend, I attended a wedding, and the theme was red roses. There were thousands of red roses everywhere! At the end of the evening, I was encouraged to take home as many roses as I could. The centerpiece consisted of at least 6 dozen roses. It was massive! That night, I arranged vases of red roses all over my house! WOW! I encourage you to use the power of visualization in every aspect of your life.

How do you want to look? How do you want to feel? Let yourself bring these images into your mind frequently throughout the day to keep you connected to the radiant self you are cultivating. Allow yourself to dream big! When you don't stand in the way of your own visualizations, the Universe will feel free to bring you great things. Trust me. Things are possible for you through the power of visualization, but you have to allow yourself to believe and hold fast to what you want.

Practice doing your visualizations first thing in the morning and then make them part of your bedtime routine as well. Starting your day and ending your day by connecting to this practice can be very potent. These two times are so important because your brain goes through various brainwaves:

The first is Beta, where you are fully awake and alert. This state is associated with worry, stress, fear and other negative emotions. Most people spend their time in this state.

The second is Alpha, which is the first layer of the subconscious mind and the gateway for advanced focus, creativity and relaxation. Mind chatter slows down and you become calmer and more peaceful.

The third brainwave is Theta. This is a deeper meditation and near sleep stage. It is a trance-like and deeply relaxed state. This is where you tap into advanced problem solving, insight and intuition.

Delta is the final brainwave. This is the deepest mediation and it's associated with deep, dreamless sleep. It helps with the immune system, rejuvenation, and longevity. It also restores your health.

When you are falling asleep or just waking up, you are in the 2–4 brainwave stages, and this is the secret sauce in programming your subconscious mind with new material that reflects the new you! Make it a daily practice to hone in on your desired outcome during these critical times – as you are starting to wake up or falling asleep. Visualize your goals and feel the positive emotions of having already achieved them. This is a game changer!

Visualizing and connecting to your big dreams through-out your day, will also help keep you inspired and engaged. You can keep your eye on the prize and open to the Universe to provide great things for you. Decide to accomplish your desires in an effortless way. Allow the Universe to bring everything that you decree to be true in your life. This can be a healthy body, an object or a loving partner. Dream big! Allow it to come to fruition as you feel love and gratitude in advance of everything you asked for, already delivered!

The Necessary Steps for Visualization:

- Be VERY specific.
- Leverage as many senses as possible (sight, smell, taste, touch).
- Feel that it's already happened and be grateful.
- Let it go. Believe that it's on its way… It's already done! If the thought of when/where/how it will arrive gets activated, STOP immediately. It's none of your business.
- Take deep breaths, get peaceful and activate your heart center of LOVE. RELAX and TRUST and LET GO. You only need to do this one time for this specific desire. You don't need to

repeat it multiple times, because the Universe has heard you loud and clear. Assume it's done and go on with your day!
- Behave like the person you are becoming. Act as if the outcome has already occurred and you are already the person that you imagine to be or have.

Be Willing to Accept Your Gifts

The Universe WILL provide, but here's the thing: You must be willing to receive the gifts that will be brought to you. This may sound counterintuitive. Of course, you would accept a big gift all wrapped with a bow when it is presented to you, right? The truth of the matter is that most people I've worked with reject gifts from the Universe left, right and center! Most people don't feel WORTHY of receiving the amazing gifts that are being presented to them. If you don't feel worthy, you will block the gifts being offered or completely ignore them. Keep that in mind. Not only are you setting yourself up for the present but also for your future.

Your mind and your body are always communicating and dancing together as you navigate through your days. Let's examine how sometimes your thoughts can literally show up in your physical body, and how you can help yourself to feel (and look) your most radiant self!

- *I AM radiant.*
- *I AM brilliant.*
- *I AM inspired.*
- *I AM bright.*
- *I AM awake.*
- *I AM magnetic.*

For bonuses go to ...

The Power of Your Body

Your body was designed as a perfect biological mechanism that has the power to heal itself. There are many conversations around this, but we are going to focus on how your thoughts can affect your body, specifically when it comes to your physique. One of the main blocks to a glowing body that you may continually face is major self-criticism when you look in the mirror. As mentioned before, changing your mindset to one with more self-acceptance is great for your mental health and it makes you feel more powerful and radiant, but did you know that your negative thoughts can actually change the way your body looks physically? For example, if you say to yourself that you "need to lose weight," you will always be trying to lose weight. Why not say to yourself that you "need to get leaner?" Or better yet, start telling yourself you're already leaner! You will start getting leaner. Don't ever underestimate the power of your WORDS. This is an excellent opportunity to use your imagination and start to visualize yourself in a lean, healthy body! Just do it. You have nothing to lose and everything to gain!

When you have deep acceptance for your body, you will experience the possibility of maintaining a healthy weight. You will come about this state of being with more ease. On the other hand, when you are under mental and emotional stress, your body is sent a signal from your brain to store more fat. This is the reason it can be so hard to maintain a particular shape, especially when your mind is in a negative state of being. When you critique yourself harshly or don't accept yourself wholeheartedly, this can be interpreted in your body the same as any other stress. Your brain and biological functions don't know how to distinguish stress. It sees all your stress as the same, no matter if you are stressed about a disagreement with a coworker, or if you aren't showing your body unconditional love and are berating yourself. It is all the same to your brain and body. It really is something to be extremely mindful of. I have seen people I work with change the shape of their body simply because they began loving themselves more. That is remarkable, isn't it?

When you are able to step into a state of love, acceptance and flow, your body will respond by getting to and maintaining your ideal weight. When you take steps to respect your body and (finally) break free from the cycles of struggling to reach unattainable ideals, you will also feel more attractive because you will respect yourself. Stop punishing yourself for not reaching your health-based goals right now. There is a big difference in wanting to try harder and constantly berating yourself. Know the difference; then feel and SEE the difference in your body. This is such a major key when empowering yourself to be more radiant. I'm sure you've encountered someone who just "glows." There is always that one person who just seems to shine, and everyone remarks, "WOW! You are glowing!" Guess what? I am guessing that they really love the skin they are in. They always try their hardest but have the utmost respect for themselves and the body they live in. Who do you want to be? This is an inside job. Soon, YOU will be the one who everyone always says is glowing!

A Glowing Body

Now that we have covered the mentality required to set yourself up for success, let's dive into the other main components: diet, exercise and sleep. What you eat, how you move and your quality of sleep are necessary for you to create a true mind-body connection. Here are some basic jumping off points for each, in hopes that it will inspire you to investigate what you feel you need most help with to become your most radiant self!

For bonuses go to ...

Healthy Eating

Off the top, I must advise you to always consult with a medical expert prior to starting any new nutritional program, especially if you have a pre-existing health condition. It's very important to stay safe and healthy.

Let's first talk about food. You know the old saying, "You are what you eat?" When it comes to your food, it is absolutely true. Find a nutritional plan that you can follow. There are many to choose from, and you can refer to your family physician if you have any health concerns. The most important recommendation is to focus on fresh and whole foods. This may simply be enjoying chicken or fish, a variety of nuts, and all types of vegetables (with a focus on dark leafy greens). When it comes to snacks, one of the best options are fruits such as pears, apples and pineapple. There is always a strong focus on keeping things whole and fresh.

A Sample Plan

*Please remember that I am not a registered dietician and to consult a RD or your doctor if you have any questions or concerns regarding your diet and health overall.

Proteins: poultry (chicken, turkey), fish and seafood, eggs, dairy products (milk, yogurt, cottage cheese).

Healthy Carbs: oats, sweet potatoes, quinoa, pumpkin, buckwheat, beets.

Leafy Green Vegetables: kale, spinach, cabbage, beet greens, watercress, romaine lettuce, broccoli.

Healthy Fruit: grapefruit, pineapple, avocado, blueberries, apples, pomegranate, mango, strawberries, lemons.

Drink 8 glasses or more of water (add lemons).

Breakfast: Mainly protein and vegetables – Omelets, bacon and eggs, and tomatoes are some examples.

Morning Snack: Fresh fruit

Lunch: Mainly vegetables – Add protein and leafy green vegetables. Or you can add carbs if you need to. Example: salad (kale, spinach, celery, avocado, cucumbers, feta cheese) and grilled chicken/fish. Additional carbs can be rice or quinoa.

Afternoon Snack: Nuts or seeds (with no added salt or oils) – If you have nut allergies, you can substitute with dairy, such as Greek yogurt and blueberries.

Dinner: Protein, leafy green vegetables, and cooked or raw vegetables – An example would be grilled vegetables (bell peppers, zucchini, onions, squash, carrots, mushrooms, and asparagus) and a small portion of protein.

Limiting dairy, carbs and sugar is best when trying to connect to your body in a radiant way. This includes the importance of limiting or cutting out alcohol as well. Trust me, you will feel and notice a difference when you limit these foods in your regular day-to-day diet.

Fasting for one day a week can also be an option to give your body an opportunity to heal and rejuvenate itself. It can help reduce inflammation, level off hormone levels, boost cognitive performance, support weight management and improve overall physical wellness. *(Always consult with your doctor before embarking on a mini fasting regime)*. An example of a fast can be solely eating fruits and vegetables for a day, along with only drinking water.

There is also intermittent fasting, which can be practiced daily. Intermittent fasting is essentially fasting for a certain number of hours during a 24-hour period, then eating and drinking only within the allotted time slot. (For example, you may fast from 8 p.m. to 12 noon the next day; then eat only during the time between noon and 8 p.m.) Many people find this very effective for weight loss.

When diving into a new diet or way of eating, remember that it takes 21 days to develop a habit. Try your hardest to stick with it for at least that 21-day period to create a definite change in your life. But be gentle on yourself. Remember that we don't want to create undue stress, so if you mess up, that's okay! Tomorrow is another day. You can restart the next day. The most important thing is to stay healthy and love your body!

Growing up, I had such a sweet tooth. It didn't help that my mom worked in a cookie factory; she would bring freshly baked cookies home every workday. I finally called it quits when my pants were getting snug. I stopped eating cookies, and after that pivotal 21-day duration, I didn't crave them at all. I had absolutely no desire for cookies, and it felt like I took my power back!

Another very important element to great health is WATER. Hydrate, hydrate, hydrate! Drinking the minimum recommended 6–8 glasses a day is always a nonnegotiable. Adding fresh lemons to your water also helps your digestive system. Your body needs this to function properly. Drink more if you begin working out more (i.e., sweating more), and get yourself a nice refillable water bottle that you love, and make that bottle your new best friend!

Weight Scales

I highly recommend refraining from weighing yourself daily. Check your weight either weekly, bi-weekly or monthly. I dislike the scale because there have been days when I really tried hard to eat healthy and also exercised, but to my sheer disappointment, the scale didn't move—or worse, I gained weight! This challenged my ability to stick to my health plan. Nowadays, I barely use my scale; I take stock of my weight by the way my clothes fit.

Exercise

I was never really interested in regularly exercising or being exceptionally physically fit. I never thought about it, and it was certainly never a priority in my life. Well, thank goodness for my son, who is somehow the opposite of me! It was a cold and wintery Boxing Day, several years ago, and I was just lounging around and enjoying my vacation time. I wasn't the least bit interested in venturing off to the gym on that cold day, but somehow, he convinced me to go to the gym with him. Okay, he did practically drag me there, but wow, I am sure glad he did! I could not imagine my life now without physical exercise. Going to the gym made me feel so good, I even started getting up at 6:00 a.m. to go work out before I went to the office. I still can't believe it! I had never in my life been a morning person, but I trained my body to get up early and I reset my internal clock.

I noticed some major changes when I began incorporating fitness regularly into my schedule. My energy levels surged, and I gained more mental clarity. I had a greater feeling of overall wellness and positivity. I lost some weight and felt stronger and more fit all around. My clothes fit better and, all in all, I just felt amazing. Incorporating fitness into my daily routine is nonnegotiable, and this is what I know to be true: If I can do it, YOU CAN DO IT!

Bottom line, moving your body a minimum of 3 times a week, for at least 20 minutes, is essential for your overall well-being. This encompasses so many things, not just going to the gym. Walking is a great place to start. I recently started jogging in the morning. I got inspired by getting involved in a fundraiser. I committed to running/jogging 10K for charity. After accomplishing this, I can't tell you how fantastic I felt. I decided to implement running several times per week. I love the endorphin boost!

Basic weight training and cardio can be incorporated into your fitness regime too. There are so many free resources online where you can do research and find what really works for you before making major investments.

Yoga Practice

> "Yoga is the artwork of awareness
> on the canvas of body, mind, and soul."
> – Amit Ray

I am sure you have heard of yoga. Yoga helps restrain the mind from focusing on exterior thoughts. It helps to reach a state of pure consciousness. The three core focuses of yoga are physical posture, breathing exercises and spiritual connection. Yoga has many added health benefits, such as improving physical strength and flexibility, boosting heart and lung function and enhancing psychological well-being. Practicing yoga can be a great addition to your physical exercise regime as its benefits are quite varied.

Flexibility and strength improve mobility and reduces body pain. Breathing exercises improve oxygen diffusion. Increasing the blood flow is especially beneficial for those with weak heart muscles. This practice can also positively impact your mental health and is thought to assist in improving symptoms of depression, stress and anxiety disorders. Research in the advantages of yoga is ever evolving. The bottom line is, it is a way to exercise, reflect and relax.

If you don't already have a regular fitness routine, just start where you are and MOVE. Get curious, have fun and you will start reaping those benefits sooner than you can imagine.
(I highly recommend that you speak to your doctor before starting any new exercise regime. Please be mindful and safe.)

Sleep

We all have a different relationship with sleep. You may have no problems with your sleep, or perhaps you and sleep are in a "complicated" relationship. It is common knowledge now that sleep is absolutely essential for both your mental and physical health. There are many books written about the benefits of sleep. For now, I want to set you up with some foundational ideas so that you may connect with the importance of sleep in your life, starting today, or should I say tonight. Remember, the goal is to get about 6–8 hours of deep, uninterrupted, restful sleep each night.

For bonuses go to ...

A big aspect of sleep is the quality of your sleep. Even if you find you don't have a hard time falling asleep, the quality of your sleep will be the game changer.

Developing a bedtime routine is the first step. Your body needs an opportunity to unwind after your day. Also, if you keep a consistent routine, this will also act as a signal to your body that it is time for sleep. Here are some very simple and effective ideas:

- Take a warm shower or have a hot bath before getting into bed for the night.
- Prepare a nice, hot cup of herbal tea that you love, and which also contains herbs that promote relaxation (e.g., chamomile or lavender).
- Limit caffeine and alcohol intake during the day.
- Cuddle up in bed and read an interesting book for a while.
- Listen to calm music that feels relaxing and soothing while you get ready for bed, and perhaps even while you tuck in for the night.
- Engage in a meditation practice that helps you calm your mind and let go of the day (you can even do it right in bed).
- Avoid screens and blue light prior to going to bed. It's possible for the light emitted to interrupt natural sleep patterns.
- Get some exercise during the day.
- Make your room dark, cool and quiet.
- Invest in a comfortable mattress and bedding.

As you can see, there are many ways to piece together a bedtime routine that works for you. If you feel like you are starting from scratch, don't sweat it. Stressing about it is not going to help. Be gentle with yourself and be willing to try things. I know that you will be able to find something that works for you, but you must be committed to trying to create this change in your life. All you have to do is show up and trust the process. Having a great night's sleep is your ultimate feel-good fuel. Quality sleep has also been proven to help speed up weight loss. This piece of the puzzle is worth investing in if you want that GLOW.

Feeling & Looking Magnificent!

In my life and work, I feel that every single thing I do can contribute directly to how I show up and glow in the world. I want to offer you some ideas that you may not have considered that will make you feel and look amazing. Sometimes it really does take shifting things in your physical world so that you can shift things in your energetic world.

There are many simple and affordable things you can do to help you feel more confident when you look in the mirror. Do you love your haircut and style, or is it the hairstyle that you have had for years, and you just ask your stylist for "the usual?" What if next time you asked for a recommendation of a cut and style that really complemented your facial features and, at the same time, tried to evoke a feeling or look you want to achieve? Hairstylists are the experts; and believe me, I bet yours would have some great ideas if you were willing to change things up a bit. It may be time for a change!

I love when my nails are manicured. It makes me feel more confident and put together. When was the last time you gave yourself a manicure, or went for a professional manicure/pedicure? This is such a great way to get some pampering in and make yourself look fresh and feel good too. You don't even have to get a color polish! Ask for clear or no polish; that works too! (I really admire men who take time to look after their nails as well!)

For bonuses go to ...

How about your skin? Do you have a skincare regimen that you not only like but makes your skin feel and look great? Investing in a facial skincare program within your budget is important. Trust me, soap and water DOES NOT cut it. Once you invest a bit more time and resources, your skin will transform. If you have a proper skin care routine, you will be amazed at the improvement you will see. Look in the mirror and even think to yourself, "Wow, my skin is glowing!" Wouldn't that feel good?

Now if you have some expendable money in your budget, you may want to consider investing in some treatments such as facials, massages and other spa-like experiences for your body. These types of luxuries may cost more than you have thought you wanted to invest in the past, but you will soon come to understand the way they make you feel: like a million bucks! Remember, when you feel good, you will also look good. Never doubt that you are worth the investment.

Creating this foundation in your physical body, through exercise, food, sleep and really investing in some self-care, will pay off. You will feel that you glow from the inside out. Not only will you notice it, but those around you will notice that you are radiating! You can cultivate peace of mind, and you will feel empowered and ready to keep growing into your best self. You will become irresistible in every single way!

When you begin loving yourself and leveling up in all aspects of your life, the world will come a knockin' at your door…and who knows who may be on the other side. Maybe it is the partner you have always dreamed of!

Chapter 2 Takeaways:

- YOU ARE ENOUGH!

- Visualization is a powerful tool to help you bring yourself into a positive mindset.

- The more self-acceptance you have, the more you will feel and look great.

- Cultivate healthy eating habits that focus on whole and fresh foods.

- Staying hydrated (especially when you are active) is key to feeling good in your mind and body.

- Incorporating fitness into your daily routine will help you feel more energetic, gain more mental clarity and foster a better relationship with your physical body.

- Committing to enough sleep is essential to your overall health.

Chapter 3

I AM SMITTEN:
Managing Personal Relationships (and Beyond!)

*"To acquire love ... fill yourself up with it
until you become a magnet."*
– Charles Haanel

How many times have you had conversations with your friends about relationships in your life, be it romantic or business relationships, friendships or relationships in your family? Really, this is what we talk about, analyze and, at times, attempt to "figure out." So, of course, I needed to dedicate a whole chapter to your relationships. The relationships you have in your life should contribute to the feeling of you being POWERFUL. However, you may experience them as taking away your feelings of power. We will definitely dig into this and discuss how you can ensure your relationships enhance your life and NOT bring you down.

Before we begin, I am just going to throw a major truth out there that I want you to come back to again and again while you are reading. Many of us want some quick fix or blanket solution to our relationship problems. There is one major secret that you need to know before you can begin working on your relationships:

The secret to creating extraordinary relationships with everyone in your life is to love YOURSELF unconditionally, tremendously and irrevocably.

Truly, this is the key. All relationships you have in your life are direct mirrors of the most important relationship of all: THE ONE YOU HAVE WITH YOURSELF. There is no denying this and no way of getting around it. It starts with your mindset. Keep all thoughts of yourself positive. Cultivate a deep appreciation for aspects of yourself such as your good health. Perhaps you have an amazing talent, such as the ability to remember people's names or a sharp, witty sense of humor. Whatever you focus on, refrain as much as possible from clouding your thoughts with negativity. This only attracts more of the same. Challenge yourself to think positively all day, every day. It is important to resonate with this fact as we explore further...

Importance of Your Romantic Relationships

When you think about your romantic relationship or partnership, does it make you feel stressed out? Or does it make you feel grounded and secure? Maybe a bit of both? Throughout this chapter, I want to talk mainly about our romantic relationships so that we can dissect this important aspect of our lives. (However, keep in mind that these recommendations can also apply to platonic relationships too!)

There is a reason that we talk about them so much with our friends! We are constantly analyzing them by going through all these feelings and trying to manage them. I would love to shine some light on important factors that you may or may not have heard of.

Relationships enrich and enhance your life and make you feel more alive. They help you grow and discover more about yourself. They support the essence of who you are fully. Relationships may also challenge you to examine yourself. This is a very important aspect of our inner beings that we are not really taught but learn as we get older and become involved in deeper romantic relationships. Recognizing and accepting ALL parts of your personality that you may not be aware of, and may not like, is reflected in relationships. They help you understand why you behave in certain ways, and they can act as an opportunity to break negative patterns. When you connect to this part of yourself, you'll make better choices when selecting the right partner.

It's also important to focus on your partner's strengths versus their shortcomings. Just as keeping your thoughts positive when you think about yourself, it is important to do the same when thinking about your partner. When you first met, you were likely enthralled by everything you learned about them. The relationship you were cultivating was exciting and interesting! You experienced new adventures, fun and laughter. As the relationship grows, it is important to continue to bring new experiences into the mix. It can be going on vacation together to a new destination, cooking a new cuisine or watching a funny film. There are so many possibilities to choose from. Get creative! Also, complimenting your partner as much as possible each day can make them feel seen. Making people feel important and special is a very loving and kind gesture, and it will boomerang right back at you.

Understanding what's right for you and what makes you happy is important! There are two options: You can struggle in your relationships, even though they don't offer any real hope of happiness, OR you can learn to see the challenges you are currently experiencing in finding your perfect match or improving your current relationship. These are opportunities to create a completely new concept that fulfills your heart and soul. I think it is obvious which would be more fun and make you feel more powerful all around! Let's strip things back a bit and talk about your self-esteem and self-worth—the most powerful seeds for a great relationship.

For bonuses go to ...

Self-Worth and Self-Esteem

We have a limited time on this Earth! Making the best of it and having fun along the way is essential, don't you agree? How you think, feel and behave affects every aspect of your existence. This is why I really want to touch upon how you see yourself. Self-esteem is measured by the way you think and feel about yourself. You can see it in your level of confidence when being met with challenges or setbacks, and your belief in your own ability to thrive and succeed.

Early in your life, your self-esteem developed through experiences such as learning how to ride a bike or getting good marks in school. People who cared for you celebrated these accomplishments and helped raise your self-esteem. Even when setbacks occurred, you were encouraged to improve in order to do better next time. As you grew into becoming a young adult, you gained more independence and then increased that self-esteem within yourself. This isn't the case for everyone. Even if you had positive reinforcements as a child, you may have developed lower self-esteem if you didn't understand how to support yourself coming into your adulthood.

People with low self-esteem struggle with self-doubt, low confidence and emotional independence. This may cause you to remain self-focused. It feels more difficult to look outside of yourself, to be present in your life and to enjoy present moments with your loved ones. So, could you imagine if you regularly feel lower self-esteem? This doesn't really set you up for success in a relationship. Relationships require you to show up, and it can be hard to do that if you are self-focused. Can you think back to a time where you experienced this within yourself, or perhaps had a partner that suffered from low self-esteem and how they did or didn't show up?

Low self-esteem involves a lack of confidence in a person's ability to be and do what they desire. It hinders their personal and professional relationships. When you have low self-esteem, you are constantly afraid of making mistakes or letting other people down. You may become a "people pleaser" because you seek approval and need to feel validated. This can often lead to other people taking advantage of you. I witnessed this firsthand with one of my clients. He sought approval from a person he was trying to develop a romantic relationship with. When she called and asked for his help, he would immediately drop everything to chauffeur her everywhere, and even dipped into his credit cards to pay for luxurious items in an effort to win her affection. When the money ran out, so did she, and it left him heartbroken. It's also very important that you don't preoccupy yourself with the wrong person. You end up exerting your energy with the wrong person, and the right one passes by.

No matter if you suffer from low self-esteem (or perhaps have someone in your life who does), I am glad you are reading this right now! I must ensure that you know YOU ARE WORTHY. You are worthy and deserving to attract and retain your perfect partner. But it starts with YOU. Your thoughts, feelings and actions are very powerful. Treating yourself with love and respect are nonnegotiable, as this is how you signal to the world that you are enough. From here, you will attract not only incredible things, but you will also attract an incredible relationship into your life.

When you operate from a place of love and kindness, first to yourself and then out to others, the Universe will get the message loud and clear. It will deliver great things. You must trust yourself and nurture a positive dialogue within. Your inner speech, thoughts and feelings reflect back to you in the way people treat you. Therefore, your intimate relationships will mirror your inner self. If this is a new idea to you, please be gentle with yourself. The possibility of growing into a wonderful person whose self-esteem and self-confidence is through the roof, is absolutely possible for you! Start with feeling worthy and deserving of the best, even if you have to "fake it 'til you make it." There is no wrong or right way to build up this important part of yourself. Once you start to master this area and begin to really love yourself, including those parts of you that you're critical about, watch out! A smitten relationship is on the horizon!

Don't forget to use your affirmations frequently during the day:

- *I AM worthy.*
- *I AM loveable.*
- *I AM confident.*
- *I AM kind.*
- *I AM captivating.*
- *I AM smitten!*

Acting as if It Has Already Occurred

One of the most important things to take with you as you continue to not only navigate through this chapter but the whole book, is this:

The frequency of love is the highest and most profound vibration.

I feel it is so important to remember this time and time again. When you work on love, you work on your whole life! This is why conversations like the one we are having are so important.

Not only will it deeply affect your love life, but it will deeply affect your *whole* life.

A great mishap that many of us make when trying to attract the perfect relationship to us, is that we often contradict ourselves with our thoughts. Remember how we mentioned beforehand that it all starts with how you feel about yourself. Let's bring that into clear focus again. I want to put it in the simplest terms for you, so you really hear me.

If you feel unworthy of love, then you will attract partners that treat you the same way. They will not respect you or prioritize you. However, if you focus on self-love and nurture these positive emotions, you will attract a partner that treats you exceptionally well. This is what I mean by contradicting ourselves! When you feel unworthy of love or don't love and respect yourself, and expect someone to show up and love you, it simply doesn't work. It actually can't! It's against the way the love vibration works in the Universe.

When you act as if love is already in your life, through showing up to not only those around you but to yourself in deep love, you will receive it: LOVE. Continue to make sure that your actions mirror what you want; and get ready to receive with open arms. The Universe will deliver!

Soulmates

Soulmate relationships are one of the greatest gifts you can receive in this lifetime. Firstly, I want to ensure that we look at this type of relationship from all different perspectives. Soulful relationships may be romantic, platonic, intimate or spiritual. A soulmate has a deep impact on you. This person can also be someone that ignites strong feelings of love or anger. I feel that many of us tend to just think of a soulmate only as a romantic partner, but that is not what I am solely focusing on here. Let's break it down a bit.

A soulmate is a person with whom you have a deep connection. There is mutual respect, unconditional love and a total understanding between you. Communication between you and your soulmate will certainly be heightened. When you are in a soulful relationship, you can be 100% yourself and the other individual will respect your thoughts and wishes. Through thick and thin, they will be right by your side because there is a strong foundation of trust, love and understanding.

For example, I have a soulful relationship with my youngest sister. We have a very strong connection and often finish each other's sentences. When we think of each other, it is often followed by a phone call. We don't have judgements or expectations, and we love each other unconditionally. We love and respect each other's families also. I treat her young daughters like I treat my own children, and she does the same. My sister and I are there for each other in stressful times to listen with kindness and offer support and good advice.

Anger is also a strong emotion that gets ignited between soulmates. This happens because soulmates face many challenges. Anger typically stems from frustration and change. When a soulmate is not prepared to make changes that would be better for the relationship, this will create feelings of upset. An example of this is if one individual is a workaholic and fully dedicated to their job. Their partner may act in anger due to the limited time they have to spend together. Sometimes soulmates will depart from each other for a short period of time due to their anger. During the time apart, they realize how important their soulmate is to them. They let go of their anger and obtain control over their emotions. Soulmates don't always learn their lessons when they are together. They may need to learn them while apart.

Kindred Spirits

Two kindred spirits together have a special connection and share a strong bond that will make their life experiences incredibly impactful. They represent the other half of the soul. They have an exceptional purpose of cultivating healing and both emotional and spiritual growth. It feels like a partnership with someone who can support and honor your spiritual journey, and you theirs. Sometimes you are able to establish an instant recognition of a soulful connection with a particular individual. And sometimes it may be a connection that develops over time. Some relationships are easy and effortless while others require an enormous amount of work and energy. This is just the way it goes! There is no right or wrong path to travel with your soulmate.

There are many signs that will confirm whether you've met this person. The moment you meet, you have instant recognition. You will feel safe and peaceful in their presence. You share similar interests and beliefs, and you see and feel things similarly. Because you are in a relationship with them, you learn more about yourself and gain a bigger perspective of who you are. Your instincts are acute, and you can feel when they need you most. They motivate you to be and do your best. You also complement each other, and everything seems easy and natural when you're around each other. You feel very connected to them even when you're apart, and you miss them when they are away from you.

When trying to determine if your relationship is strong, ask yourself: What was it exactly that first attracted you to your current soul relationship (or one from the past)? What compelled you to want to know this person more? Hold the answers to these questions close as the relationship plays out. This comes in handy, especially during those rocky times with your romantic relationships. There is a reason that you connected with this person and wanted to stay... Maybe a good course of action would be to stick around and see what happens.

Remember: You know you have found your soulmate when you accept a person as they are and don't try to change anything about them. It may take work, but believe me, it is worth it! This may be one of the best experiences of your life.

Twin Flames

According to Greek mythology, humans were originally created with four arms, four legs and a head with two faces. Zeus was the primary ruling God and feared their power. He decided to split them into two separate parts. These two separate parts vowed to search for their other half throughout all lifetimes, and thus created the most profound love connection.

How will you recognize your twin flame? You will feel intense emotions. There's a strong magnetic connection and this person just feels "right," and you feel safe. You have many similarities and you both have a desire to grow and evolve to higher levels. The meeting of your twin flame generally signals a major change in your life for the better, as they can cause radical personal awakenings for each other. They complement each other and the relationship is very intense. They also keep coming back together because they feel like they're home.

Twin flames are also physically drawn to each other. The sexual connection is very strong, and they feel blissful and peaceful at the same time when they're together. The physical energy is overwhelmingly intense, and undisputable. Kissing is considered spiritual and ignites a rush of emotions and strengthens the bond of love, trust and intimacy between them.

I had a friend find her twin flame, and it is an interesting story! She saw his pic on a social media site and felt an immediate attraction to him like no one she's ever met before. After they connected on that platform, they decided to meet in person. She said the first meeting was exciting—like teenagers going on a date. They got to know each other over lunch and, before leaving each other's company, he gave her a big hug. As their hearts touched, she immediately realized they shared a huge connection. Their connection was very strong physically and emotionally. They continued seeing each other over a period of time, until eventually they decided to be in a more permanent relationship.

Karmic Relationships

Karmic relationships are needed in our lives because they offer an opportunity to grow from past unresolved issues. These relationships can be the most emotionally challenging. There is definitely an instant recognition between these two people—they initially feel a strong connection. They can also feel frustration, because their other half can be happy one moment or unpleasant to be around the next. There's often drama and miscommunication, and typically a lot of highs and lows and turbulence. Karmic relationships may also feel addictive because they are constantly drawn in for a reason. This relationship teaches the ability for tolerance and personal preferences in a relationship,

For bonuses go to ...

and while they often start as a whirlwind, they can end just as quickly. The purpose of relationships like this in your life is to teach life lessons.

- *I AM soulmate.*
- *I AM witty.*
- *I AM ecstatic.*
- *I AM connected to my love.*
- *I AM united with the love of my life.*
- *I AM elated.*
- *I AM romantic.*
- *I AM affectionate.*
- *I AM humorous.*
- *I AM cheerful.*

Expectations

Let's circle back to a few major highlights: accepting your partner and the feeling of being "good enough." I feel a lot of couples get into major trouble when they start placing expectations on each other. When you place expectations on your partner and on your relationship, you are saying to the Universe that what you have is not good enough.

When I'm talking about expectations, I am specifically referring to rules that you live by that originate from your core beliefs. You must let go and recognize when expectations are unreasonable. They can and will be a major roadblock on your path to finding a partnership. If you have a love relationship in your life, unreasonable expectations can lead to feeling disappointed, hurt, jealous and downright angry. Who wants to feel those things or bring that into your relationship? Having those negative feelings in your body and mind is not only doing a disservice to your relationship but to yourself as well. You will not be setting yourself up to allow positive things to flow into your life, even outside the scope of your relationship.

Notice how I said *unreasonable* expectations? Keep this in mind when sorting out how you feel. Sometimes what you expect may be totally unreasonable, not fair and are left over feelings steeped in the past. Check in with yourself, especially if you feel anger or let down by your partner A LOT. And don't forget: Communication is key! Your partner may be totally unaware of your expectations. Remember that no one can read your mind. Even if you haven't clearly communicated your expectations in the past, you must be willing to have an open and honest dialogue about them now. When communicating with your partner, it is a good practice to start sentences with "I am." For example, "I am unhappy when you tell me you will arrive at 6:00 and you show up an hour later. I feel disrespected and that my time is not valued." In this approach, you're taking responsibility for how you feel and sharing it, instead of simply blaming the other person by saying, "You're always late!" Can you see the difference? Establish some healthy ground rules that you both agree to. It may take some work at first, but any of the uncomfortable feelings will be worth it later when things are running a bit smoother. Never forget that your relationships are for growing, not for shrinking. Own it!

Establishing Healthy Boundaries

How are you when it comes to your boundaries? People are most content when they establish what **is** okay and what **is not** okay. They don't allow people to do things that are not okay, and certainly don't let them get away with it. In any relationship, be it romantic or otherwise, if clear boundaries are not set, you will get more of what you **don't** want versus getting more of what they do want.

People with no boundaries tend to harbor feelings of unworthiness, be "people pleasers" and feel the need to explain themselves excessively. If you don't clearly express boundaries in your life, the Universe will continue to give you experiences that demonstrate how you don't have boundaries. Without clear boundaries, people tend to assume that others will do things on purpose to upset them. What if people you are in relationships with are doing the best that they can? You will never really understand what is going on unless you have a discussion around boundaries with people you are engaging with in your life.

Once you've established boundaries with the other person, relationships can continue to grow in a loving and kind way. You can be authentic and more trusting toward other people as well. This changes the energy in your life to fill it with more kindness and compassion.

There are 6 human values that we need to feel in order to show up fully in life:

- Feeling significant (special)
- Having certainty
- Being connected
- Contributing in some way
- Personal growth
- Being aware of uncertainty

Once you become clear on which values are important to you, then you can set boundaries based on actions that you feel may not be in line with the values. When you can be vulnerable and express clearly what you want, you can be authentic and prioritize yourself. This changes how you show up in the world.

If you are not used to it, setting boundaries can feel like a foreign practice and very uncomfortable. Here are three foundational ways that you can clearly define and set your boundaries with the people in your life. These can be the jumping off point to incredible new relationships or help strengthen existing ones.

1. Speak your truth. You must authentically express yourself and your truth.
2. Learn to say NO. When you say no to something, you say yes to something else. If you keep saying yes to something you dislike, you will enforce that cycle.
3. Be clear and identify what your needs/values are. This will really clarify and establish your boundaries.

Here are some affirmations to help enhance your stipulated boundaries may include:

- *I AM authentic and clearly state my boundaries in my relationships.*
- *I AM in a significant, loving relationship where we share what works well and what we need to improve on.*
- *I AM in a mutually loving and beneficial relationship with my significant person.*
- *I AM comfortable having regular touch points of open dialogue with my significant person about our relationship.*

Negative People

How do you manage dealing with difficult or negative people in your life? Oftentimes, you will get triggered by their negative attitude and respond back with similar negative energy. The best way to handle these interactions is to respond back with kindness and a peaceful demeanor. Be firm but kind, and don't get pulled into the drama. This will often settle down another's anger because they certainly don't expect it. Most importantly, you can maintain your inner harmony by not taking their negative "bait." Nobody can take away your positivity without your consent! Ultimately, by responding from a place of compassion, you will help to transform their negative state to a positive one.

Negative people harness fear and require more love than the average person. When faced with a negative person, challenge yourself to come up with half a dozen positive aspects of them. Send them positive loving energy and picture them engulfed in a bright light of happiness and peace. Never allow negative people to take advantage of you with their temper tantrums, crying or other bad behaviors. Refuse to contribute to their selfish agenda and stay true to the Divine essence of who you truly are—a spiritual being, living a physical experience.

Intimacy

Now on to a more fun topic! What is a love relationship without intimacy? Well, not much at all if you ask me, or millions of people! Paying attention and ensuring there is intimacy in a relationship is VITAL. It can set up your relationship to continue to grow and be nurtured. Without it, relationships wilt, sometimes beyond repair. Kissing, tender touch and being close are all important to the overall health of a relationship. It is how you share intimate love with one another.

Communicating your needs to your partner is crucial. When you are willing to show up and both your needs are met, you and your partner will feel seen and loved. Your relationship will feel nurtured, and your bond will only strengthen. You will share a resiliency to any stormy weather you may encounter because you will feel that you have each other's back. I know you are busy. I know your partner is busy. We are all very, very busy people! But even small acts of intimacy, like a kiss hello or a hug at the end of a long day, will sometimes be all you need. Trust me. Like the saying goes, "Little things mean a lot," even when it comes to being intimate in your love relationship.

The Five Love Languages

In order to be smitten, it is important to understand what your partner requires to feel treasured in a relationship. In the book *The Five Love Languages*, Gary Chapman shares the 5 ways that romantic partners can feel special in their relationship by how they express and experience love. These are:

- Words of affirmation
- Quality time
- Receiving gifts
- Acts of service
- Physical touch

It is very important to know your partner's love language(s) and use it to strengthen and improve your relationship. You can inquire further online and take the test to discover your preferences. My love languages are words of affirmation, physical touch and receiving gifts. However, the trick is in knowing that people will often execute their preferred love language on others. My husband is a perfect example of this. He always performs "acts of service" for me because that's his love language. For example, he fills my car with gas regularly without me asking him. This is a very unique experience we share because I have to admit that I have never filled my car with gas in all the years we've been married. When I tell people this fact, they're shocked. Because I know his love languages, I will find ways to perform acts of service for him as well. And in turn, he will also be mindful of my love languages such as physical touch by ensuring he always gives me a nice hug when he comes home from work. When you know each other's love languages, it can be a beautiful dance of connecting with them in order for you and your partner to feel special and seen.

Attraction

What makes you attracted to someone? What makes you attractive to others? When you are interacting with someone, this is your first insight to what intrigues you about that person. It is a signal for you to PAY ATTENTION. There may be something there for you. When you want to shine a bit brighter for yourself and for others, there are a few things you can keep in mind. Your posture and the way you walk can send a message that you are confident and feel energetic. Others will be attracted to it. Another way to sparkle is to not take yourself too seriously. Learn to laugh at yourself! This is another simple yet powerful way to exude confidence.

There are a few other ways you can increase the attraction factor between you and another. Making as much eye contact as possible when speaking and listening can feel amazing. Take notice of their eye colour and how much eye contact you actually have with others when talking. There is a difference! When you engage in more eye contact, this can spark passion in one another. While we are on the subject, another way to intensify passionate feelings is to engage in an activity together where emotional arousal is high. This can look like participating in something where you may feel more fear and excitement, or even a physical activity, such as a roller coaster ride, skydiving or water sports. When adrenaline is being produced, there will naturally be more connection with another person.

And what if you are already engaged in a relationship? There are many small and meaningful ways you can show a person that you remain attracted to them without needing to spell it out. Always take the time to tell them you respect and admire them for something they accomplished. It may seem small, but your acknowledgement and words can mean the world to someone. An interesting "hack" that I like to use is asking the person you are involved with to do a small favor for you. Perhaps they can drive you to an appointment or pick you up. When it is genuine and not done from a sense of obligation, it creates an unconscious motivation to like you more. Interesting! Can you reflect back on when it was the other way around and you did someone a favor, but not out of obligation? Maybe you cooked someone a delicious meal and they thoroughly enjoyed it? How did that make you feel? It may have pleasantly surprised you.

It reminds me of when my mother always cooks a Greek dish made with homemade pita bread and feta cheese or spinach for the family. She makes it with love, and we devour it with excitement just like small children! She feels great making a dish that we enjoy. I always say that she has golden hands. Her baked goods cannot be replicated!

No matter what stage of a relationship you are in, be it early days or further into a connection, making time for each other as much as you can is necessary. When you are in a good mood, it is even better! If you are in good spirits, you will be able to remain present and celebrate each other's company. However, when you are in a bad mood, it can often feel like a cloud is looming over you. Sometimes it is okay to just take your own space and then spend time with that special someone when you are feeling better. This can be especially helpful early on in relationships. Showing up as your best self can make things more fun and offer an opportunity to connect.

Any relationship you have with another requires constant attention and effort as it evolves over time. A relationship will also present personal challenges and opportunities for growth for both parties involved. Successful relationships only exist when there is a strong foundation of respect, forgiveness, honesty, understanding and self-esteem. Building great relationships takes effort! But if there is a mutual intention to nurture what you have, this will strengthen the connection of love. If both of you are committed to cultivating a great relationship (not just riding it through), there will be no end to the powerful possibilities of what the relationship can hold!
When you change your mindset, you will begin to set the foundation for living in the highest vibrational frequencies possible. It is achievable and feels incredible. What does "living in a high vibrational frequency" actually mean? In the next chapter, I will explain it all and empower you to take the next steps in your powerful life!

Chapter 3 Takeaways:

- Romantic relationships enrich and enhance your life and make you feel more grounded.

- Your relationships can act as mirrors of how you see yourself.

- When you act as if there is already love in your life, you will remain open to receiving love.

- Setting clear boundaries enhances your relationships and your life as a whole.

- Stay positive and do not fall victim to others' negativity.

- Connect and repeat your affirmations throughout the day: I AM Worthy, I AM Loveable, I AM Confident, I AM Smitten!

Chapter 4

I AM A BOMBSHELL:
How to Achieve
High Vibrational Frequencies

*"Vibrate so high,
and radiate from so deep,
from so much within your heart,
from your essence, from your soul,
so that no one can come close to you
without destiny's blessing
in their hands."*
– Butterflies Rising

Have you heard the saying, "Good vibes only?" Yes, it may feel like it is simply a saying you see on a t-shirt or coffee mug, but as we have touched upon through the book, there are actual "good vibes" in your life. To be clearer, everything that exists has a vibrational frequency, and frequencies run low to high and everywhere in between. The higher a vibration is, the better it is for you.

When working on becoming a more POWERFUL person, it is important to begin aligning yourself on a higher vibration and vibrating higher yourself, from the inside out! This isn't something that necessarily happens overnight. Achieving a higher vibrational state can take some time, and there are many ways to access it. I want to share with you some of the methods that I know of and have personally tried that work.

You may be asking yourself, "How will I know when I am, or others are existing in high vibrational frequencies?" When one is in a high vibrational frequency, your inner light shines brightly, and you appear to be glowing from the inside out! You look happy, peaceful and sparkly. You just look more attractive to others for some reason and, many times, people are not sure why. You will be a "bombshell" and you won't even have to try!

Improve Your Character, Raise Your Vibration

Generally speaking, how do you show up to the world? Do you walk out your door with optimism, strength and energy in your step? Or do you drag your feet and bring a heaviness wherever you go? As we have examined throughout the book, how you show up in the world can reflect what the world will give back to you. You will attract the energy that you put out there. Take some time to take stock of how you are showing up to your life, as you may understand with more clarity why your life is working FOR you or AGAINST you. When you are able to maintain high, positive energy, you will attract similar people and things into your life.

Working from the inside out is key! Start with how you feel as you go about your day. The goal is to be in a state of joy and optimism most of the time. Notice if you are able to easily pick yourself back up when you get knocked down, and how you generally respond to everything in your life, be it in your personal life or at work. Having a sense of humor is essential! When you are able to see the lighter side of life, you will feel a sense of ease from the inside out. And this sense of ease will allow you to connect back into feeling positive. Don't take yourself or things around you too seriously! Let your hair down and enjoy the ride.

Living as the most authentic expression of you is profound. It will get you in alignment with higher vibrational frequencies quickly and effectively. Sitting in your authenticity starts with knowing your self-worth and letting that grow to a place where you unconditionally love yourself. Oftentimes, it feels easier to love those around you than to turn that loving inward. But at the end of the day, you need to be your own champion, biggest cheerleader and best friend. When you love yourself, your relationships with those around you will change for the better. Be it with your professional colleagues, family, friends or partners, setting healthy boundaries is a way to show some love to yourself. (Please, never let anyone treat you like a doormat! You deserve better.)

Operating from a space of deep self-worth will also help you set your priorities and execute your goals with passion and excitement. This feeds back into energetically staying in a positive space. Whether it be your career or a personal focus, starting with feeling worthy of trying will go a long way. Then jump in, get excited and look forward to the challenges that life will inevitably give you.

How Confident Are You?

Sure, some of you may feel that this is easier said than done. If you aren't sure where to start in feeling more self-love and self-worth, perhaps you can start with your general sense of confidence. Feeling more confident is possible through your physicality. Take stock of how you stand and your posture. Do you tend to hunch forward and close yourself off? Or do you connect to standing tall and proud with both feet planted on the ground? This can open you up energetically, but you will also just LOOK and feel more confident. Be willing to make eye contact with people around you, especially with people you come into contact with. This keeps you open to a positive energetic exchange. Smiling as well can help lift your spirits and in turn increase your confidence and overall higher energetic vibration. Think of all the ways you can keep your body language open and welcoming. It is then that you will continue to keep the door open to the positive energy that is seeking you. Stay true to yourself!

Train Your Mind to Think Positive

We just touched upon the importance of being joyful, optimistic and having a sense of humor. However, I know that at times this is easier said than done. I want you to know that it is not just YOU. Your subconscious mind can play into how you act in your day-to-day life. Your subconscious mind has been programmed to think in very specific ways by negative messages that exist all around you that you may not even be aware of. So, when you find yourself struggling with things like low self-esteem, lack of discipline, addiction and other contributing factors exuding a lower energetic frequency, understand that it is very possible that this is a reflection of what your subconscious mind has been programmed to play out.

Deprogramming your subconscious mind is possible and necessary in order to break through some bad habits that may be holding you back from stepping into a place of great confidence and high positive frequency. It is like you have been hypnotized without you knowing it, and it is time for you to take charge of your mind again. This is a process of empowering yourself that takes courage and time, but it is worth every ounce of energy that you have.

To begin the process of deprogramming the subconscious mind, it is necessary to go back and identify when the program was introduced and formed. You can then begin the process of reprogramming into a new desire that you wish to cultivate. For example, oftentimes, low self-esteem is programmed into our subconscious in our childhood. Perhaps you were not supported when you had interesting ideas, or maybe you were told to just be quiet and not be as expressive as you wanted to be. Whether you liked it or not, these ideas to act "smaller" were literally programmed into your subconscious and, as an adult, it will show up as having low self-esteem and not feeling confident.

If you want to cultivate more confidence as an adult, you have to recognize this and make a connection with it. In fact, it can be shown that most problems and issues we experience as an adult were formed as a result of our childhood traumas and negative experiences. Recognize that a little YOU still lives inside your adult body, and all the things experienced as a child have trickled into your adult life. This includes all the negative experiences. But it is possible to DELETE the old subconscious programming and replace it with NEW programs that will support you in raising your vibrational energy.

One of the easiest and most effective ways to do this, is to start acting in a way that aligns with the new YOU that you are cultivating and bringing forth. This is where being mindful of how you are going about your day-to-day business becomes imperative. Staying in a positive energetic space physically will not only help you in the present moment, but it will also help you reprogram your subconscious mind. When you do that, you will then be setting yourself up for success in the future.

The Power of Self-Talk

The entry point for reprogramming your subconscious is your self-talk. Begin observing how you speak to yourself on the regular. What is your inner dialogue? Is it supportive, loving, humorous and positive? Or is it berating, insulting and negative? Your aim is to slowly but surely correct that self-talk to something more supportive and positive. This is where your change will be rooted.

All the affirmations we have been exploring throughout the book can be helpful, especially ones that are rooted in boosting self-confidence:

- *I AM confident and beautiful.*
- *I AM a bombshell!*
- *I AM intelligent and I express myself with ease.*
- *I AM a genius!*
- *I AM loveable and I AM loved.*
- *I AM fearless.*
- *I AM sexy.*

These affirmations are just the starting point in helping you boost your positive self-talk. You are the CEO of your life and need to learn how to truly motivate yourself. Whatever has happened in the past is over. Focus on all the vast future possibilities for happiness that exist ahead.

Ensure that you are speaking to yourself in a manner that is uplifting and observe what words you are using as well. For example, if you are trying to think about a new goal and are saying things to yourself such as "I should" or "I'll try," you are going to be setting yourself up in a loop where you are constantly trying to reach your goal as opposed to saying **"I AM."** All the language that you use for self-talk will be programmed into your subconscious—every single word. I know this may sound daunting at first, but creating these changes is possible. Believe in yourself and work through it step by step. When working through this program, remind yourself that it was the "old you." You are not that person anymore! You are the BEST version of yourself now. You are making new decisions because you are the queen/king of your new life now.

Never forget that your self-talk is linked to the Universe! What you say out loud or in your mind, you will create because the Universe will make it so. You are constantly in a relationship with the higher energy of the Universe. Using the affirmations throughout this book is a powerful exercise in creating that connection, and a great starting place, especially if you feel a bit lost. Self-talk is such a fantastic way to raise your vibration.

Once you get the gist of what I am talking about, it won't take so much mind power. It will become a feeling and an internal understanding as to when you need to shift. When you combine positive self-talk with positive emotion, nothing will be able to stop you! You will gain the confidence to start thinking BIG for yourself and your life. You will see that you are truly a powerful force and have everything you need to achieve your goals and dreams. And it all starts in your mind and stays in a higher vibrational state.

Increased Endorphins: Feelings of Happiness

Can you think of a time where you felt genuine happiness or joy? How did you feel inside? Feeling a sense of joy or happiness is key when thinking about getting into a higher vibrational frequency; however, you don't have to wait for something to happen to you. You can produce endorphins through your own actions!

For bonuses go to ...

Endorphins are the "feel good" chemicals that get released into your body when you do specific tasks either mentally or physically. It is very helpful to know how to produce endorphins on your own so that you can be more mindful of ensuring you work on things that do. It is especially handy on days where you may feel you need a "boost" in your life. On the days where your mood is feeling a bit lower, knowing what you can do to help yourself feel a bit brighter can help keep you in the higher vibrational frequency.

First thing you can do to release some endorphins is to move your body in an intentional way. Have you heard of people getting a "runner's high?" Well, that is exactly what it is! It refers to the endorphins that are produced after going for a run, and the feelings that flood your body in return. Now, you don't have to go for a run if that is not your cup of tea. Any time you do some sort of exercise, endorphins will always be released. Going for a walk, taking a yoga class, dancing to a fun tune or going for a bike ride all count as well. Just move your body!

Connect with Loved Ones

Making time to connect with people that are important to you is invaluable. I'm sure you have a list of people in your life that you love talking with and when you leave their presence, you always leave with a smile. Having meaningful connections with those we love keeps our positive energetic frequency high. It is a reciprocal relationship as you contribute to others raising their vibrational frequency as well. Don't forget about your furry friends! Taking time to play or have a cuddle with your pet can instantly make you feel more relaxed and put a smile on your face. And don't forget that your partner or romantic relationship can be a great source of positive energy. Taking time out of busy schedules to connect is essential. It can look like sharing some coffee in the morning and having a heartfelt conversation. Or perhaps making time to be intimate. When you connect with your "number one person" in a focused and meaningful way, endorphins will assist you to feel lighter and more at ease. Keep all those that you love close, and always make time to connect.

Surround Yourself with Joyful Things

Everything you bring into your environment can have an impact on how you feel and how positive your energetic frequency will be. Sometimes small things can make a great impact. Take for example having some candles burning in whatever room you are in. You don't have to save candles for a special occasion! Allow their warm glow to create an atmosphere no matter what you are doing. I love having some candles in every room so that I can enjoy some candlelight no matter what I am doing.

Essential oils are a powerful and fun tool you can have wherever you go. Each oil has its own properties that you can utilize for specific applications. For example, lavender oil is commonly used for its relaxation properties, while peppermint may be used to invigorate your senses. You can harness the power of different oils' properties, but you may also just be drawn to a particular scent because it makes you feel joyous or uplifted! This is what you want, to feel good when using an essential oil. It is fun to investigate the different ways to use oils; but truly, one of the simplest ways is to place a drop of the oil of your choice on your palm, rub your hands together and then take a nice inhale of the scent. Take a moment to enjoy the scent and how it makes you feel. You can also add some drops of essential oil to your diffuser and enjoy the scent throughout your home.

When I talk about your environment, I also want you to think about your environment outside! Taking a walk in nature is amazing medicine. Many of us now live in more urban environments, and with that comes overstimulation of our senses—too much noise, too many flashing lights… just too much! And whether you know it or not, your energy is greatly affected. Getting out in a more natural setting can help recalibrate your system. I am sure you have had an experience where being in nature has almost instantly made you feel more calm and relaxed. An integral aspect of being outside more is also getting out into some sunshine. The sun can give us an automatic energetic boost. Think about how you feel when, after several cloudy days, you wake up to a sunshiny morning. There is no other feeling like it! The sun's energy naturally makes us feel more positive, alive and optimistic. And it's just outside your door waiting for you.

Feed Yourself Positivity… Through Your Belly!

Do you ever think about how the food you eat can help you feel more positive? Our food decisions and how we decide to nourish our body will also play directly into how high our vibrational frequency will be. It makes sense, doesn't it? The healthier your food is, the greater chance that good food will feed your mind and mood. Focusing on a nutritious diet is key. We covered this in a previous chapter, but it is such a valuable topic and worth noting again as it correlates with achieving high frequency! Supporting your body by eating enough protein will also help your energy. It is easy to add more protein that includes high quality beef and chicken, eggs, nuts and legumes. Always take a look at what is on your plate, and ensure you are eating some protein every time you have a meal or snack. Do you enjoy spicy food or tend to shy away? There is something about eating high intensity food, such as something spicy, that activates your body and mind in a very specific way. It is invigorating!

And of course, we can't forget about the pleasure of eating dark chocolate. The health benefits of eating high quality dark chocolate have been brought to people's attention before. But have you ever associated it with bringing higher positive energy into your life? What a bonus! Treat yourself to some really good dark chocolate soon, savor every bite and notice how you feel. What a delicious experiment...

Other Ways to Increase Your Vibration

There are many other small but mighty things you can do to take care of yourself, and in turn take care of your energy:

- **Complete a task off your to-do list.**
- **Celebrate the small wins in your life.**
- **Watch a comedy and have a good laugh!**
- **Listen to uplifting music.**
- **Read an inspiring book.**
- **Challenge yourself to learn something new and build a new skill.**
- **Ensure you get adequate sleep and rest.**
- **Have genuine, authentic connections with others.**
- **Connect to a meditation practice.**

This is a great jumping off point. I encourage you to hone in on and add things to the list that are personal and meaningful to you.

Raising your vibrational frequency may have sounded daunting at first, but I am sure you can now see that it is all about taking good care of yourself and those around you. When you do, you will easily exist in a more positive energy state. Continuing to focus on raising your frequency day in and day out can only bring amazing things into your life. Remember, like attracts like! Every change and commitment to your well-being, no matter how small, will make an impact.

Now that we have discussed how to raise your energetic vibration, I think it is a great time to swing back and look at your life as an individual. The next chapter is perfectly timed. We are going to examine how you can live a life that is fearless! When you work on living a life that is fearless, in conjunction with everything we have been discussing up until this point, you will begin to set the foundation for living in the highest vibrational frequencies possible. It is achievable and feels incredible. In the next chapter, I will explain what I mean and empower you to take the next steps in your powerful life.

Chapter 4 Takeaways:

- Living at a higher vibrational frequency is essential to being a more POWERFUL person.

- Reprogramming your subconscious mind is necessary in order to create deep seated change when facing things that can lower your vibration, such as low self-esteem.

- Things that make you feel good will set you up for attracting good into your life.

- Moving your body intentionally and joyfully can release endorphins and make you feel inspired.

- Your environment and the choices you make are extremely important in how your positive energy will manifest.

- Connecting with others in meaningful ways will connect you to higher vibrational energy and help them cultivate more positivity as well (win-win!).

- Taking care of yourself in small but mighty ways is essential.

Chapter 5

I AM FEARLESS:
Living Harmoniously & Stepping Into Your Power

> *"Be fearless in the pursuit*
> *of what sets your soul on fire."*
> *– Jennifer Lee*

Fear is a part of our lives that we can't escape. No matter who you are, there is no doubt that at one point you have experienced fear in your life. Fear can be a great teacher. But the key is remembering that fear solely lives in your mind. It is an illusion that can play a trick on you and keep you living in negative thought patterns. When you think of being fearful, you may directly relate it to feeling fear of something in particular. However, one may even feel fear of things they can't see, like the past, the future and even death.

Fear of failure, fear of rejection, fear of loss of love, or fear of loss of money are all primary causes that may keep people stuck in their current environment. You may get into a comfort zone that keeps you sheltered from facing these fears, thus preventing you from stepping outside the box and creating a magnificent life.

Every aspect of your life has the potential to be affected by fear. These thought patterns can lead to toxic relationships, poor health and patterns of failure. This is why it is essential to understand what your fears are, how to face them and to learn how to overcome them. Never forget that the opposite of love is fear, so the closer you want to be to living an empowered and powerful life, the farther from fear you must be.

For bonuses go to ...

Facing Your Fear

You were born virtually fearless. Babies have two fears: the fear of falling and the fear of loud noises. But as you grew into an adult, your fears continued to multiply and stretch out over many aspects of your life. Other top fears for adults are public speaking, confined spaces (claustrophobia), heights, thunder and lightning, the dentist and snakes. As you can see, fear manages to seep into all areas of your life, from the subtle and specific, to the encompassing and grand. What fears can you identify in yourself? Maybe there are fears you have that you know well and manage in your day-to-day. However, perhaps there are some fears that are very specific to particular situations or environments, which you avoid at all costs in order to not have to face your fear or fall victim to it.

Be cognizant of getting too wrapped up in your fear! You may unintentionally create things in your mind through overanalyzing your fear, and possibly attract it into your life. Fear solely lives in your mind, and only you have the power to make it as ugly or as manageable as your imagination will allow. Don't live in the future… Stay focused on the present. If you need to seek professional help to overcome fears you are struggling with, please do it. I often reach out to my support team when needed.

When I made a commitment of living a powerful life, I also committed to facing my fears head on. I understood that I was going to have to stop them from having supreme power over my life in order to lead the life I wanted. I decided to face one fear that I knew was holding me back from feeling like a strong leader in my career, and another that I felt was holding me back from having the adventures my spirit craved.

Fear of Public Speaking

As a bank manager, I was called on often to deliver presentations in front of large audiences. It was something that I dreaded. My legs and hands would literally shake because I was so scared! Even though this was a regular part of my life, it never got easier for me, and I always found myself petrified to speak in public. There came a point where I recognized this was a fear I had, and as with all fears, it was possible to overcome it. I made the decision to not allow this fear to govern my life any longer.

I wasn't sure how to dismantle this fear of public speaking, so I sought guidance in a public speaking course. Everyone there was committed to being supportive while providing objective and honest feedback. Some people simply wanted to elevate this skill, and some people had fears of public speaking as I did. As we worked on our skills, it was always interesting to me that the feedback I consistently received was that I looked more confident than I felt. This gave me a bit of confidence. Now I just needed to match my inside to my outside.

For me, the secret was to practice reading my material in a private setting, then practice in front of family members, close friends or even a mirror, and to do all this before I even got to the podium. Being prepared enabled me to feel more comfortable, which helped me to settle some of the butterflies and be more grounded. I also visualized myself speaking confidently and everyone in the room receiving the information in a positive manner. After I finished my course, I delivered my first large presentation to 300 people, and it was well received! I even had great feedback from people I didn't know. That was the first time I had ever done public speaking without feeling rattled with nerves! My confidence was instantly boosted, and I felt empowered. If I wanted my career to continue to grow, I knew I would be faced

For bonuses go to ...

with many more public speaking engagements; and having conquered this fear made me feel empowered for my future. I could now also see how the fear of rejection is closely linked to the fear of public speaking. I noticed how the fear of rejection seemed to dwindle relative to my confidence in public speaking (something important to keep in mind!).

Fear of Heights

Until recently, another fear that I have lived with almost all my life is a fear of heights. I can trace it back to an experience I had when I was about 6 years old. I discovered a crawl space that led into our attic and, from there, I found a way of getting to the roof of our house. At the time, we still lived in Greece, and I would go out there, multiple times a day, and enjoy the view. My parents were busy working, and my grandmother didn't keep a close eye on me. I remember how happy and powerful it made me feel! It all changed when one day I slipped and almost fell all the way to the ground. Fortunately, I was able to grab hold of something and get back up. Needless to say, it scared the daylights out of me, and from that day forward, I was scared of heights.

I am a bit of a daredevil and like challenging myself as well. Several years ago, I decided to face my fear of heights head on and signed up to go skydiving. I didn't really think about it. I just did it, knowing that it would definitely be one way to force myself to take this fear on. The night before, I almost backed out! I kept thinking that it would be like a ride at an amusement park, where you drop from great heights at extreme speeds. Needless to say, I was scared, but I didn't let myself back out and I persevered. I am happy to report that not only did I go through with it, but it was one of the most exciting adventures I've had in my life! There is nothing like the experience of floating down to the ground from a plane, and the views of the world from thousands of feet up are truly magnificent.

After my skydiving trip, my fear of heights decreased significantly and is now absolutely manageable. I have even had other fun adventures that have involved heights, like ziplining in the jungle. I now have a different relationship with this fear, and never again will it stop me from not only having once-in-a-lifetime experiences but also a lot of fun!

I am sure that you have some inkling now as to a few of your own fears that you may want to take on. You may be able to really see how overcoming some of your own fears will be instrumental to opening you up to new possibilities in your life. Let me touch upon a few fears that are very common but a little more nuanced. I am certain that if you don't constantly live with one of these, chances are you have felt them at least a few times in your life.

Fear of Failure

Failure is a part of life that we cannot escape. It is reasonable that you would experience a fear of failure because, many times, the failure you may fear could cause consequences in your life. However, when the fear of failure is out of control, it will put stress on your emotional, mental and sometimes even physical health. The accumulation of anxiety, worry and indecisiveness can lead to major health issues. This is because all these things are resulting in a constant feeling of stress.

As mentioned earlier, what you think of and keep in your mind's eye, you will create. So, you are doing yourself a disservice by constantly focusing on the possibility of failure... You may actually bring it into your reality! Never forget how powerful your mind can be when it comes to creating your reality.

At the end of the day, when you are so preoccupied with failing, you will always just simply play it safe. Conformity keeps you in the high percentage of people that just lead a boring, mundane life. This is not the way to live if you want to achieve your full potential in life! As I mentioned, everyone will experience a fear of failure; however, it is successful people that **act** despite their fear. Ask yourself, "What is the worst thing that could happen?" Follow this with, "What is the best thing that could happen?" When you are able to see the outcome in both ways, usually the reward of you going **beyond your fear** is so much grander than the fear itself. Refuse to dwell on fear by forcing your mind to think of your goals and dreams and staying positive. Occupy your mind with thoughts about your dreams coming to fruition!

How would you act if the fear of failure didn't exist in your life? It takes bravery and courage! But this is the way to go if you want to step into a powerful space in your life.

- *I AM doing it!*
- *I AM courageous!*
- *I AM safe!*
- *I AM agile!*
- *I AM protected!*
- *I AM tenacious!*

When you practice this affirmation, you will feel surges of positive energy and conviction that will override the feelings of fear. If you have been carrying the fear of failure with you for a long time, it may take quite a lot of practice. However, never forget all the success and joy that is waiting for you on the other side of your fear of failure.

Fear of Aging

Another fear that I feel is fairly common is the fear of growing old. There are two aspects of growing old: the change in your physical appearance and the change in your mental capacity.

When it comes to changes in physical appearance, some people reach for cosmetic surgery, Botox injections, fillers, spa treatments, specialized exercise, fad diets and specific vitamin cocktails. It is a multi-BILLION-dollar industry! That alone speaks volumes to how fearful people are of their age actually showing. When it comes to their energy or zest for life, some people just seem to give up. They lose their overall curiosity and stop seeking out new adventures for their life. If you are relating to anything that I am saying, I want to ensure you know that you have the power to grow old elegantly and gracefully.

Aging and growing old is a powerful process of life. With each year that passes, you gain more wisdom and insight into the way life works. You get to know yourself more intimately, and the people around you, on a deeper level. Gaining this wisdom and experience is invaluable as you can use the power of your age to guide and assist younger generations. Doesn't that sound more inspiring than just living with the fear of the fact that you will inevitably grow old?

Affirmation:

- I AM ENERGETIC, MENTALLY COGNITIVE AND PHYSICALLY FLAWLESS!
- I AM HEALTHY, FIT AND STRONG!

Infuse your thoughts with powerful, youthful energy on a daily basis. Always hold a vision of yourself as young, vibrant and powerful! Affirm that you are healthy and of sound mind.

Work on visualizing yourself at 100 years old, full of sharp wit, agile and glowing with health. Never forget that at the end of the day, age is a state of mind. I know people in their 30s that act as if they are in their 80s, and vice versa. As the saying goes: "Age is just a number!"

Overcoming Your Fear

Overcoming your fears, no matter how big or how small, takes practice and courage. It is a process that cannot be balked at, as fear can be overwhelming and feel intense in both your mind and body. You will literally be working with exploring the idea of engaging your mind over matter. Let me give you some clear and simple ways that you may move forward in beginning to overcome your fears:

The opposite of fear is LOVE. When you increase self-love, self-worth and self-confidence, you will be able to take fearless action that will propel you to achieve all that you desire. In times of fear or negative emotions, always revert to feelings of love. Get into your heart center. When someone upsets you, send them love. This will disempower the negative feelings of fear.

"What is the worst thing that could happen?" By asking yourself this question, you are beginning to dismantle the fear in your mind and create a new, more manageable relationship with it. You will not be allowing it to become bigger and bigger with each moment that passes. Remember that fear is in your mind. It is a perception, and you can choose to be fearless and play out that scenario in your mind instead. This is empowerment!

Leverage the power of the Universe: Invite the Universe to assist you with your fears and worries, doubts or anxiety that you may be feeling. Don't underestimate the power of the Universe. Ask for help and know, without a doubt, help will be provided. Once you ask, let go of the outcome. Don't try to figure out how it will happen…Just let it go! Your limited mindset cannot compare to the vast Universe extraordinaire!

Program your subconscious mind through visualization: When you visualize your desired outcome and tap into feeling joyous and positive, the old fears you possess will be overridden. Your actions will then play out as you have seen them and felt them. Visualize the end result exactly as you wish it to be. Own it. Remember, it takes a minimum of 21 days to retrain your mind and for these positive intentions to penetrate into your subconscious mind. Stay the course!

Fear doesn't exist: Give up dwelling on fearful outcomes. It's exhausting and painful. Your imagination is conjuring up those fearful predicaments because you're in conflict with yourself. You are human and everyone makes mistakes. We are all human after all! Stop thinking about it and LET IT GO. Intentionally think of something positive instead. Be stubborn about reverting to a wish-fulfilled mindset instead of dwelling on useless fear.

DO IT: Step up to the plate and take action! You must be willing to jump in and take a risk. Think outside the box! Challenge yourself to do something every day that makes you feel fear. You will start to feel more empowered and will diminish your adapted fears.

Talk about your fears with a good friend, spouse or a psychologist or psychiatrist if necessary.

Hypnotherapy is also an option to explore. The treatment deletes negative emotions from your past. You will remember the event, but you will not feel the negative trigger. (It is imperative that you find a qualified practitioner if you choose to go this route.)

Act "As If"

Another very powerful tactic you can try is acting "as if." It is a practice that will lead you to success. Act AS IF you are already confident in what you are doing. Act AS IF you do not possess the fear that you feel. Start to FEEL the opposite of your fear. Get into the feeling of the wish being fulfilled. Act AS IF it were impossible to fail.

Execute your dreams confidently and with courage. This is an opportunity to develop this craft of overcoming fear so that you may begin to lead the life of your dreams.

An essential part of this process, of course, is your affirmations. I encourage you to create some that are specific just to the fears you are tackling.

For example, you can then affirm:

I AM HARMONIOUS.

When you maintain a harmonious mindset, fear cannot exist. All affirmations will penetrate more effectively in this calm state of being. There are no fear-based conflicting messages when you operate from a harmonious mindset.

You can also start with a more general affirmation that sets you up to begin to tackle individual fears more successfully:

I AM CONFIDENT.

See yourself as a more confident person when facing any fears and as you go about your day-to-day life in general. You don't shy away from a challenge and are comfortable stepping up to the plate, be it personally or professionally.

With all your affirmations, remember to repeat them to yourself before you go to bed and when you wake up in the morning. Pair this with your visualizations and tapping into the feeling of successfully overcoming your fears, and you will notice great changes in your life as each day goes by.

Meditation for Eradicating Fears

Here is a clear step-by-step meditation you can practice daily to help eradicate any specific fears that you may be working with. This can be a great place to start for any fear, big or small. You will see how easily adaptable it is for anything you need to manage.

For bonuses go to ...

This visualization is so powerful, and it only takes a few minutes!

- Close your eyes and bring yourself into a calm state.
- Take 3 deep breaths in through your nose and exhale through your mouth.
- Continue focusing on your breath.
- Go deeper. Count to 10 and, with each count, allow your body to relax even more, from the top of your head down to your toes. Keep letting go until your entire body feels completely relaxed.
- Imagine a beach...a vast blue sky...a deep turquoise ocean.
- Feel the warm sun on your skin.
- Hear the waves cascade over the beach.
- Hear birds chirping happily.
- Smell the salty water and beach air.
- Feel completely relaxed in your comfortable, cushiony chair.
- Allow your entire body to feel light.
- There is nothing to do and nothing to think about.
- You are on the beach in a calm state.
- Feel the peaceful energy.
- Feel completely safe in this happy place.
- State some I AM affirmations while you're in this peaceful state.
- Get into your heart center and feel love as you state your I AM affirmations.
- I AM peaceful. I AM harmonious. I AM fully supported. I AM calm. I AM courageous. I AM love.
- When you are ready to come out of this place, count to 5 and open your eyes.

When you feel fear, just bring yourself to this space. You can choose any scene that you prefer. You can be in a forest, the mountains or anywhere you feel the happiest and most calm. Remember to incorporate as many senses as you can—feel, smell, hear, see, taste. The more you do this exercise, the easier it will be to get to this state.

When you commit to practicing meditations such as the one above, you will be programming these new feelings of fearlessness into your subconscious. You will be altering your subconscious by deleting the fearful programming and replacing it with a fearless update! It is so powerful, and I cannot wait for you to try it!

When you work on living a life that is fearless, and all the other amazing mindsets that we have been discussing up until this point, you will begin to set the foundation for living in the highest vibrational frequencies possible. It is achievable and feels incredible. Let's take a deep dive into your personal life and how you can harness the law of attraction (and beyond!) to help empower you to realize a life you love.

For bonuses go to www.elenigiakatis.com

Chapter 5 Takeaways:

- In order to lead a powerful life, it is essential to face and overcome your fears, no matter how big or small they are.

- In order to live a powerful life, you must face your fears head on.

- Fear will inevitably affect every single aspect of your life, from your health to your relationships, to your work and overall well-being.

- You have the power inside you to overcome all your fears.

- Ask the Universe for help in your journey and it will support you.

- Always use your affirmations to help in the process of overcoming any and all fears.

Chapter 6

I AM THE CREATOR OF MY DESTINY:
Leveraging the Various Laws to Attract Everything in Your Life!

> *"What you think, you become.*
> *What you feel, you attract.*
> *What you imagine, you create."*
> **– Buddha**

When you look ahead to the life you want to live, what do you see? Do you have a vision of what you want your life to be like? Or do you feel disconnected; maybe even lost?

How about your present life? Do you really understand how you are spending your time and, more importantly, your energy? Can you see how these things are connected?

When looking to **create** your future, it is important to understand where you are and where you want to go. I love thinking back to when Thomas Edison invented the lightbulb. He had extreme linear vision! It took him years to have a successful invention, and he is quoted as saying, "I haven't failed—I've just found 10,000 ways that it won't work." What a powerful analogy that demonstrates relentless vision. He believed so strongly in his goal that he wouldn't stop until he accomplished it.

When looking at creating your own destiny, it is essential that you have this particular sense of focus and drive. And not only is it important for you to have a clear vision of your future, but you need to have a clear sense of your present as well. Know exactly where you are starting from. When you can hold both your starting point and your destination in your mind, you can then clearly drive your life to your goal. You will also set yourself up to leverage the power of the law of attraction.

For bonuses go to ...

The Magic Happens in the Present Moment

Being in the present moment is one of the most treasured states of being. This is where the magic is! This is where you receive help to execute your desires. When you are in the present moment, you can maintain a high vibrational state, and THIS is where the juiciness of creation lies. BUT it's not always easy!

The Secret Ingredient!

If you learn to stay in the present moment, with a feeling of joy and love within your heart, you will get *so good* at achieving your most succulent goals that you will feel like a magician! Everything that you desire in a present and high vibrational state will come easily and in divine time. Things will just seem to fall into place, but it's actually your energy and your vibration that makes it so.

At one point in my career, I was working as a junior bank advisor and decided that I wanted to move into a senior role. It involved taking extensive financial planning courses so that I could be qualified. However, at the time, I was raising two young children and the cost of the courses wasn't in my budget. I decided that my employer should pay for the courses upfront since I would be upleveling my skill set and, in return, providing greater value to the clients that I worked with. I was extremely passionate about this path and knew that it would all work out for everyone involved if I could get the course paid for outright.

My manager could only offer compensation after I successfully completed all courses, and to me, that wasn't an option. There was a strict protocol that covered compensation for courses within each pay grid. My manager's authority didn't cover exceptions from this guideline. I decided to one-up (with her permission) and wrote a very compelling letter to the VP, and to my delight, it was approved. I completed all the courses, received my new accreditation and directly went to my manager asking to be promoted to a more senior role. She looked at me and said that she was dreading this day: the time had come to move forward in my career. She didn't want to see me leave her team, but she was awesome and connected me with our human resource department. I got an interview and was hired right away! My journey in elevating my career is a powerful example of deciding to move forward and asking for what I needed in order to get to my goals.

I must tell you, there was no doubt in my mind that my employer would co-operate and I would move forward. Why? I used the law of attraction to my advantage. I **asked** for what I knew I needed in order to move forward. I **felt** as if I had already received it and that this was the right path. And there was no doubt in my mind that I would **receive** it. This then paved the way to **allow** it to unfold without interruption. Knowing to ask for a promotion after my studies were completed, not only made it clear to my manager that I was ready to move forward, but it also made it clear to the Universe. I will talk more in depth about how I leveraged the law of attraction in my career specifically, in a later chapter. For now, let's take a look at the law of attraction itself: what it is, how it works and how it can dramatically change your life. When you harness the power of the law of attraction, you will truly be the CREATOR of your destiny!

What is the Law of Attraction?

The law of attraction is one of the most powerful laws in the Universe. I know that may seem like a very grand statement, but

For bonuses go to ...

I stand by it! The law of attraction encompasses the idea that every thought vibrates and radiates a signal, and every thought will attract a matching signal back to its source (you!) It may seem like a simple concept. It is... and it isn't. Let's really break it down so that you can feel empowered on how to use the law of attraction for your own well-being and creating your own destiny.

Boiled right down, the law of attraction can be thought of as **like attracts like**. It is magnetic energy that pulls toward you and your desire. The key to attracting something into your life is to achieve vibrational harmony with what you desire. You not only do this with your **thoughts**, but you do this with your **feelings** as well. I mentioned that your thoughts send vibrations that can act as signals. YOU must be in vibrational harmony with what you want in order to attract it. This looks like keeping your mind on what you want and then also feeling as if you already have it. You really have to harness the power of your imagination for this, through joyful thoughts. You must pretend that what you want (no matter if it is an object or experience) has come to fruition. When you continue to practice these thoughts and emotions repeatedly and consistently to increase your vibration, you must then ALLOW this item or experience into your existence.

Let me give you a simple example. Make it fun for yourself! When I first started connecting to this practice, I would calmly and peacefully manifest receiving flowers. I would picture a beautiful bouquet of flowers. I would then ASK for them and feel like I had already received them. Then I would KNOW without a doubt that they would arrive. After going through this process, I would let go and trust the Universe would bring them into my life when the time was right. To ensure I would keep the "ask" at the forefront of my mind and expedite the process, I placed a photo on the screen saver of my phone so that I would constantly be reminded to feel amazing about their arrival! It is imperative that you feel and believe in your mind that it has already happened. If you have an opposing thought of the item not arriving, delete it immediately and refocus on the feeling of the wish already being fulfilled.

It was fun to witness various flowers coming into my life in different and unique ways! For example, one time my husband went grocery shopping and surprised me by bringing home a beautiful bouquet of flowers for me. Another time, I received a beautiful bouquet of flowers from my colleagues. Even my little niece picked some flowers from the garden and brought them to me. Flowers were showing up everywhere! I thanked the Universe for bringing them to me and continued to believe that it would happen again and again... and it did!

Practicing managing your thoughts in this way can be tricky at first, especially if you are in the habit of thinking only about things you DON'T want. This is something you must be aware of and manage properly. The law of attraction doesn't know the difference between things you want and don't want. It operates solely on the vibration of your thoughts, no matter what they are! Don't forget that like attracts like, even if it is something you do not desire in your life!

I see this time and time again with people I work with. It is much too easy to get stuck in thought loops about things you DON'T want, and then watch as those things consistently become part of your experience. It makes sense! This is the law of attraction, and it works with whatever you are thinking and feeling. It doesn't know the difference. So, if you are constantly thinking about how you are financially unstable and feel "broke," this isn't going to bring more money into your life! It will keep you where you are as you will be attracting the thoughts and feelings of lack.

Now what if you made a few adjustments? What if you were to acknowledge the abundance you have in your life now, create a vision of what you want in the future (i.e., more money), and by using your imagination, are able to feel that sense of financial freedom within you? Now, THIS will attract the abundance into your life. See how it changed from attracting what you do not want, to what you actually desire?

(I can't wait to do a deep dive into this specifically in the next chapter!)

The bottom line is, nothing can occur in your life experience without your invitation by your thoughts and your feelings. Always keep in mind that positive thoughts far outweigh negative thoughts; therefore, positive thoughts and feelings have a much higher frequency than negative thoughts and feelings. When all is said and done, you are creating your reality whether consciously or unconsciously. So, stay very connected to your thoughts and feelings. Working on this can, and will, change your life.

Recognizing a Blessing in Disguise

It's also your responsibility to protect your positive energy and high vibration. It is easy to get pulled into a negative state when you're listening to an irate person complaining. When you've disconnected with this person, you'll need to take a few deep breaths, relax and reconnect to the present moment and a calm state of being. Again, it is about learning how to stay open to what the Universe has to offer you. Negative experiences, no matter how big or small, help you grow. Sometimes they are gifts in disguise.

Ask yourself WHY you may have become upset. What triggered these emotions? If you can listen quietly, your internal guidance system will offer the answers. This is an opportunity to let go of those emotions and triggers that no longer serve you. You get to dissolve the old emotional patterns (a download from your past) and choose a new path, one that is filled with joy and prosperity. When you're able to pinpoint a trigger that stimulates a negative emotion within you, you can begin to dissipate it and start the healing process.

I have seen people turn their life completely around and even break cycles of addiction by understanding their triggers. A friend of mine had an alcohol addiction. She drank because she often felt that she couldn't move forward with her life, goals and aspirations. I assisted her in getting some help and to identify the reason for the addiction. I am happy to say that she is now completely sober, in a loving relationship and has joined the workforce. I'm very proud of her determination to change her life in a profound way. (Addiction is not always easy to conquer on your own. There are many resources available, and I always recommend getting professional help to overcome addictions and move forward in your life.)

The Art of Surrender

After you have asked for something and aligned your feelings with that vibration as well, the third layer of using the law of attraction is to ALLOW. What do I mean when I say that? I mean to allow the Universe to flow steadily and unrestricted into your existence. When you don't resist the flow of the Universe, it naturally, easily and joyously brings you all that you desire.

I find that surrendering can happen when you are in a more relaxed state. I often meditate or listen to relaxing and soothing music in order to bring myself to a place where I can be present and accepting. This especially helps when I am feeling upset or impatient!

Have you ever displaced something important, like your keys or your phone, and just can't find them? I'm sure you have had times where you have turned your house upside down looking for them and couldn't locate them. The feeling can drive you crazy! You feel frustrated, and sometimes it can even make you feel angry. This is a great example of when it is best to learn to relax and allow the Universe to help you out. When this happens to me, I decide to fully disengage from the frenetic feeling I am in and fully relax. I decide that whatever I have lost will turn up in its own divine time. I connect to the feeling and believe wholeheartedly that it will turn up. Then I let go by leaving it in the Universe's capable hands. And wow! It always works! Whatever I have lost will come back into my view or appear somewhere. It always fills me with such delight, and I thank the Universe. Can you think back to a time where you were able to accept and allow something to come into your existence, and watched it become a reality?

To ensure you are fully empowered to begin working with manifesting and the law of attraction, I want to take everything we have been discussing and break it down into three clear steps. I want you to be able to not only engage fully with the process but hold yourself accountable for keeping in line with the vibrations that will add goodness to your life, not bring yourself down. You are more POWERFUL than you ever thought possible!

- *I AM trusting.*
- *I AM serene.*
- *I AM calm.*
- *I AM spirited.*
- *I AM grounded.*
- *I AM free.*

The Process of the Law of Attraction

1. Ask and you shall receive.
If you are curious about self-development, I'm sure you have heard something along the same lines in the past. And the bottom line is this: If you don't ask, you will not receive anything, no matter how big or small. The first step is to always ask. However, when we are talking about the law of attraction, it isn't quite that simplistic.

The major component of this step is *feeling* worthy. You must deeply feel your worthiness when connecting to the powerful Universal flow. This allows things to flow toward you from a vibrational standpoint. If you also connect to a feeling of being blessed, you can expect good things to flow toward you. You don't resist when gifts are presented to you. (Gifts can look like opportunities, synchronicities, etc.) If you feel UNworthy, you will block important things from coming into your life. This is just the way this universal law works!

Yes, asking for things with words can work, but how you align yourself with particular vibrations through your feelings is most powerful. And it doesn't matter where you are starting from. You may be ill, bankrupt, jobless, etc., but no matter where you are, you CAN start from there. You have the ability and POWER to start creating NOW!

I also recommend that when creating new possibilities for your life, to keep your goals private. Of course, you will want to share a new idea or feeling of freedom that you have found, but oftentimes when we share our goals with others, they may express skepticism, which then can lead to creating doubtful thoughts, fears and frustration. It is easy then to start doubting yourself and questioning your own abilities to create your dreams, and you can't harbor those feelings if you want to remain vibrationally aligned with what you want. Makes sense, doesn't it? Keep your dreams and goals as private as possible and make the journey a personal one.

2. It is given.
Never, never forget that the Universe is vast and abundant! Your desires may be given, your prayers may be answered, and your questions/requests may be fulfilled. I know that if you are new to working with the law of attraction, it can be difficult to really connect to the idea that the Universe is infinitely abundant, but the truth remains the truth.

The size of your desire or request doesn't matter. What counts is how you **feel** on the receiving end of things. You must be in the state of being where you already have that which you desire. The timing of gifts given are directly linked to your feelings of worthiness and your biases. What do you think would be easier to obtain: a chocolate bar or a thousand dollars? You can obtain BOTH! It will just depend on you and how you approach what you are asking for. If you feel that the chocolate bar will be easier and quicker to get, and the thousand dollars will be much more challenging and will take a long time, then that is how it will play out. You will feel whatever truth you choose into existence.

I urge you to take some time and examine how you have been feeling about things you are looking to receive from the Universe.

Take a good look to see if you have been feeling as if things are hard and laborious, or if you have a sense of ease and possibility, no matter what you are asking for. This will be a huge insight as to why you may be waiting much longer for your big desires in life... much, MUCH longer than needed!

3. Allowing.
This is the final step of the process of attracting what you desire. Tuning your vibrational frequency through your thoughts and feelings to match that of what you want is nonnegotiable. You must learn to get really aligned! However, that alone won't seal the deal. You must ALLOW what you are asking for to enter your life. You have to think of it like putting yourself in receiving mode. When you are in receiving mode, EXPECT to receive what you are calling in. This completes the manifestation process that you are creating with the law of attraction.

Makes sense, doesn't it? How can you actually receive what you are visualizing and feeling, if you are not open to it? It would be like feeling deserving and asking someone for something and then keeping your hands closed when they offer it to you. You have to keep your hands open with the Universe. In order to keep yourself open to allowing great things to flow toward you, use the tool of visualization. Visualize things coming into existence before they get there, and you will remain on the same vibration with more ease and be more open to receiving. You will feel more attuned to understanding when the Universe is trying to help as well.

The three parts of working with the law of attraction are essential. I feel the best place to start from is to really understand your emotions and create a strong relationship with your feelings. The bottom line is, **you will know exactly where you are headed by how you feel.** Your heart and mind must stay laser focused on what you want, not the sense of lack. I know we already touched upon this, but I must bring it up again! Why? Well, take for example the people in my life constantly saying they can't afford things. They often say they can't afford the bigger house, or a vacation, the luxurious car of their dreams... They send the sense of lack vibration into the Universe and their lives, and then they blame their *circumstances* for all the lack. It doesn't occur to them that they have created these circumstances by their negative thoughts! That is the way the law of attraction is designed—it brings to you what you think and feel!

You Are the Creator of Your Destiny

I know for many of you, the above statement may feel like it is coming from way out in left field. This may not be the way you were taught to think of things or how you feel right now. Even though it may feel awkward or odd at first, it would be extremely helpful if you take time to accept the fact that you are a vibrational being and you live in a vibrational Universe. And there is no escaping the fact that there are laws (like the law of attraction) that govern the Universe.

When you feel connected with universal laws and gain understanding of why things respond the way they do, your confusion will be replaced by clarity; doubt and fear will be replaced by knowledge and confidence, and uncertainty will be replaced by certainty and joy!

Don't get stuck swimming against the current! When recognizing that you are in a negative thought, delete it from your mind immediately and begin your I AM affirmations. Empower yourself with your words. Think of everything you want and use the words I AM in front of these desires (as we do with everything in the book!) If you desire more financial freedom, repeat "I AM wealthy." If you desire a healthy body, repeat "I AM healthy." If you desire a better relationship, state "I AM soulmate."

Other Important Universal Laws

As it is imperative that you really understand the law of attraction, I want to briefly introduce to you several other universal laws that are important to be familiar with. These laws can be implemented into your life in so many ways. I encourage you to do more research on them and understand how they can help you empower yourself.

The Law of Relativity

Everything that exists in your life is relative to something else. One million dollars may seem like a lot to one person, while to another it is not. A 5000 square-foot house may feel too big for one person, but to a person who is already in a 25,000 square-foot home, it would feel small. It is all about PERCEPTION. The way to leverage the law of relativity is to be cognizant of your perception. Minimizing issues that you are facing is important. It all happens in your mind. Learning to understand how to shrink the energy of issues as if you had all the resources in the world, and not giving them as much importance, will aid in growing your self-worth. When you feel more self-worth in your life, you will attract your desires more quickly and more peacefully.

The Law of Cause and Effect

Have you heard the phrase, "You reap what you sow?" It serves as a reminder that we are always in the driver's seat. You create everything in your life with your thoughts. When you are able to change your thoughts and emotions, you will most definitely experience a different outcome. You are not a victim. Shift that mindset once and for all by taking 100% responsibility for everything in your life, and then watch your life change for the better.

The Law of Polarity

Everything in the physical world has two opposites: good and evil, love and hate/fear, hot and cold... In regard to manifestation, examine what you want to create, and think about its opposite. Your deep-seated negative beliefs that are in your subconscious mind (e.g., not intelligent enough to succeed or not attractive enough to be in a relationship) will impact your intentions. If you want to be successful or in a loving relationship, your emotional energy has to be onside with your desire and intention. If you experience strong positive emotions like joy and excitement along with your intentions, your manifestations will come to fruition. It is important to be cognizant of this law, especially if you're having difficulty attracting all that you desire.

The Law of Gestation

There is a period of time that must pass to bring something to form. For example, a baby goes through a gestation period of 9 months before it's born. When you are working on yourself and achieving your goals, it will take time in the beginning. However, once you build up momentum, the period of time between the idea and attaining your goal will speed up. Be patient and realize that everything has a gestation period, even when you are creating changes in your life.

The Law of Rhythm

Life possesses an inherent rhythm. An example of this is the four seasons. Nature moves through the four seasons in a precise rhythm. You live in a rhythm when you're not rushing or doubting. Patiently observing your thoughts, catching yourself when your thoughts don't align with your dreams, and reverting back to more positive, clear thoughts of what you want to accomplish, is part of the rhythm of your life. It is a gentle way to create what you want patiently; kind of like a slow dance.

The Law of Transmutation

This law comes into play during a period of time when things are not going according to your plan. You may feel uncomfortable or feel like giving up altogether. However, you must persevere through this period and step into the unknown until you get to the other side. Transmutation happens when you're trying to create or change something big in your life. It can be thought of like a caterpillar turning into a butterfly… no easy process!

Never forget: You have the power to CHOOSE. Choose joy, happiness, love, great health and abundance! Believe in yourself and then allow the Universe to be on your team. Work together to make your life full of possibility!

The next chapter is perfectly timed. We are going to examine your relationship with money! I want to share with you how empowered you can be with the energy of money in your life, and that there is nothing stopping you from living a life of financial freedom.

Chapter 6 Takeaways:

- The law of attraction is a process that you engage your mind and soul with.

- Ask and you shall receive. It is given. Allow for it to happen.

- From an energetic perspective, being mindful and present are necessary to create change in your life.

- You can create your future with having a clear vision of where you want to go.

- Hone your skills in understanding when you are being presented with a blessing in disguise.

- Learn to relinquish your control and surrender to the power of the Universe.

Chapter 7

I AM A MONEY MAGNET:
The Power of a Wealth Mindset

> *"I am a money magnet.
> I always attract abundance and prosperity
> easily and effortlessly into my reality."*
> **– Rhonda Byrne**

Are you having financial difficulties?

Are you struggling to make ends meet?

When you think of money, do you automatically become extremely stressed and want to go back to bed or grab a glass of wine or run away and wish you didn't have to think about it?

I'm sure that many of you answered yes to these questions. The good news is that you have come to the right place! We are going to achieve a total understanding of how to increase your bank account and have all the riches that you desire! When we talk about money, we need to talk about your **mindset** first.

Wealth is a mindset. This is the truth, plain and simple. But because of the world we live in, it feels like it isn't that simple at all! Throughout this chapter, we will unpack how time and time again, YOU (and your mindset) are the biggest enemy to your own personal financial success. You and your beliefs will either create prolific abundance or poverty. How does that work exactly? Don't you need a really good job and be good at saving or investing? You could achieve some monetary success this way, but you would have to work very hard. There is definitely an easier (and more fun) way!

For bonuses go to ...

It starts with understanding that MONEY IS AN EXCHANGE OF ENERGY. I put it in all capitals for a reason. This is a truth about the world we live in, and you need to realize this immediately. Since money is an exchange of energy, you have the ability to CREATE money.

You are a creator of your life through your mindset, and this also applies to money. I AM A MILLIONAIRE—or better yet, BILLIONAIRE—is a great example of a wealth consciousness, which you need to build into your mind if you want to be a millionaire or billionaire. It will not happen otherwise. We will go further into detail about how to do that and WHY you may not have this wealth consciousness right now.

If money is an exchange of energy, ask yourself whether <u>your money is flowing IN or OUT of your life.</u> Remember, it is an *exchange*. You will not find success when you operate in ways such as hoarding. This is a sign of feeling LACK and that you believe there will never be enough, and that it's best to hold on to what you have with all your might! Sound familiar? On the other hand, when you are open to the energy flow of money and have a wealthy mindset, you set yourself up for abundance. Money flows freely and easily into your life, and there's always enough to cover your expenses, plus enough surplus cash in your bank account to save and have some fun. You can lead a life of happiness, luxury and financial freedom, and own every material possession you've ever desired (if that's what you want), OR you can continue on living in stress, anxiety, worry and guilt when you actually do spend your money on something fun. We have such a limited time on this Earth, so which feels better to you?

Take a deep breath and trust in this paradigm shift. Let's keep unpacking this mindset, piece by piece.

Give and You Shall Receive

Something you must remember always is that the law of attraction functions within the power of LOVE. This is why one of the cornerstones of creating abundance in your own life is to stay open to helping and supporting others. The law of abundance is clear:

*In order to **receive** wealth in your own life, you must first **give**.*

I know many of you are feeling that this is counterintuitive in a way. I'm sure you are saying to yourself, "But if I give, I will have nothing," and this is simply not true. It just isn't the way things work!

When you are open to the giving of yourself, whether it's through your positive thoughts, time, energy, money or overall general help, it will start the FLOW of the energy of abundance. There are so many ways to give gifts to people around you. By simply offering positive words of encouragement and high vibrations toward the people around you, you can impact other people's lives and their physical world. When giving a gift of money to someone, do so with love and good wishes. Always give money or other gifts from a place of kindness and helpfulness. It is an opportunity for you to contribute to that person's life and the world, so do so from the highest vibrational place—LOVE!

Never forget the old adage:
You reap what you sow.

Being willing to help other people to think and act abundantly, and spreading wealth when acquired to everyone around you, is acting in accordance with these laws and energies. Remember that the energy of abundance is a flow—you must give and be open to receive.

A great way to manage the energy of abundance is to give to others more than you take. If you are earning a salary, earn your income by providing a greater service than the salary value you will receive. This principle holds true in any form of payment you receive. Always give more service value than the cash value you will receive. Again, this is putting more positive, personal service-driven energy out into the Universe than what you expect to receive in return in dollar value.

If you are willing to continue to give happily, and you don't close that energy pathway down, it sends a strong signal to the Universe that you are open to receiving just as much, if not MORE, than what you give. I think this quote by Charles Haanel (famous philosopher and businessman) sums it all up perfectly:

> "We make money by making friends, and we enlarge our circle of friends by making money for them, by helping them, by being of service to them. The first law of success is service."

Never forget, the flow of abundance starts when you open yourself up **fearlessly** and believe that good things are flowing toward you. Believe that there will always be more coming your way and more to share with others.

Mental Conflict

My family comes from very humble beginnings and have worked very hard to acquire everything that they have today. We immigrated from Greece to Canada when I was seven years old. My parents did not speak English and obtained blue collar jobs.

They always struggled to make ends meet. This doesn't surprise me now as their relationship with money was one of fear. They saved desperately to own real estate and raise three daughters. I remember they constantly lived in fear of losing their jobs and not being able to pay off their mortgage debt. Every single dollar was accounted for as they continued to grasp and hold on for their dear lives.

Knowing what I know now about having an abundance mindset, I can see how my parents constantly blocked themselves from the possibility of greater abundance in their life. They held on to money very tightly, and constantly had conversations about how they never had enough or would never have enough if they didn't work hard and save. This fear around money consumed them and continues to this day. My mother still warns me that I should save more money, while I feel financially secure. She remains fearful that there wouldn't be enough money. I have a great deal of compassion for all their struggles in trying to survive in a foreign country, just the two of them, while raising a young family and trying to make ends meet. They worked very hard, and I appreciated this because it taught me discipline. However, as time went on, it took a lot of guts and perseverance to break free from a lack mindset that was constantly bestowed upon me. I have always been a bit of a rebel and questioned their well-meaning advice because I wanted to enjoy the finer things in life and not struggle the way they did.

In my twenties, I established my own goals and, each year, learned to be even more fearless. It took time and determination, but I started to achieve successful results by increasing my salary with every new promotion. I asked questions and received lots of advice from the pros around me, which helped upgrade my negotiating skills. In hindsight, I can clearly see that the best thing I did was to disregard the fear-driven advice that they gave

For bonuses go to ...

me. At the end of the day, I understood that they were trying to help me the only way they knew how. But I decided to take a leadership stance in my life by not adapting a lack mindset, and my life has transformed. I also leveraged their good advice around working diligently to accomplish my goals.

Children often learn this fear-driven mindset from their parents and carry it with them into adulthood. Sadly, when they adopt the same fearful "lack" mindset, they may also inherit the same life of struggle. Even if you didn't come from a similar family situation such as mine, you may adopt these mental blocks toward abundance, from friends, co-workers or even just the world around you in general! It is of the utmost importance that you take some time to recognize if you are holding onto some blocks or limiting beliefs, as it will stop the abundance of energy from flowing into your life, which we previously talked about. Once you understand them, it may be easy to recognize these blocks. However, at times, it may be hard to assess if you are keeping yourself open.

Start by being mindful of your everyday thoughts. How are you relating to things around you? Notice if you are constantly thinking about how there is "never enough" in your life, or if you find yourself reaffirming to yourself that you cannot manage your finances and can't afford to purchase luxurious or fun, frivolous items (if you desire them). Pay close attention to your conversations around money and how you react to them. When money gets brought up in any way and you are meeting these conversations or situations with fear or negativity, this is what will be attracted to you. By your thoughts alone, you will block money from flowing into your life. When you meet the Universe with a fear mentality, you will attract negative conditions to you. This is literally the way the laws of the Universe work.

A very common example is if you are having trouble making ends meet. It seems that no matter how much you work, you are always struggling to pay bills, or you never have left over money to just do something fun like going out for a nice dinner with someone you love. It feels like a struggle, day in and day out. In a situation like this, you have to be very cognizant of the conversation you are having with yourself. Perhaps you're thinking that there's minimal space in your budget for something like clothing. You've been eyeing a sweater, but you convince yourself that you don't need it. Or you constantly reject luxurious and pleasurable material possessions because they are not practical purchases. Look at this as an opportunity to change the conversation revolving around "not enough," to a positive one of prosperity. You will be changing your mindset and allowing more abundance to flow to you. The cringing and "aha" moments will attract great things to you.

When it comes to money in your life, I hope you see how you are *way* more in charge than you think. Ask yourself this question: Is it easier to attract a cup of coffee or a million dollars? If you feel that a coffee is easier than the money, then you are NOT thinking BIG enough. An abundant mindset would be open to attracting a million dollars just as quickly as a cup of coffee. Remember, there is NEVER a shortage of money in this world. The Universe truly is abundant and infinite… even when it comes to MONEY!

Abundant Mindset – Very Important!

Now it is clear to you that most of the work in creating more abundance in your life is all in your mind! We've taken a look at the blocks we experience and started the process of ensuring you remain open to the flow of abundance. Now we have to **nurture** the abundance mindset. You can't just sit back and wait for your million-dollar checks. You need to CREATE money by executing ALL opportunities that come your way and stay open to spotting them when they arrive. This is the most powerful recommendation! Stay open to million dollar IDEAS and execute when they appear! A wealthy mindset will allow you to identify these new ideas when they present themselves. A poor mindset will not register and that brilliant money making idea will wisp right by. This is why it is so important to dismantle the negative mindset bit by bit. Stay in the present moment and recognize negative thinking. As soon as an impoverish thought comes to mind – delete, delete, delete!

Once you have a money making idea, you can find ways to bring it to fruition. There are always Investors that are willing to partake as well as the bank that can lend you the money you need to start up.

The small percentage of wealthy people in this world have done the work to think abundantly. They feel deserving of all the abundance in their life and expect more to come on a regular basis. This is not an easy task and that is why the vast majority of people remain low to middle class. Where do you want to be?

As we have mentioned in previous chapters, some of the most important times of your day are first thing when you wake up and right before you go to bed. This is when you are either setting up your mindset for the day ahead or you are closing the day out and ensuring your thoughts are still aligned. *I AM WEALTHY* and *I AM SUCCESSFUL* are some extremely powerful words that you should use throughout your day but especially first thing in the morning or before falling asleep. Saying these potent and specific affirmations will help to draw in more abundance and success. When you say these words of affirmation to yourself, your subconscious mind will accept it causing you to feel it to be true. Only when you feel it to be true will you draw wealth and abundance to you. Again, this is the way the Law of Attraction and Law of Abundance work.

Work with these affirmations, more positive thoughts and feelings of abundance throughout your day as much as possible. These affirmations are especially useful when you feel unsure of yourself. In these situations, step up your affirmation regime!

When you convince yourself that you are wealthy, you will attract wealth. Your IMAGINATION is a powerful tool! Imagine yourself living in your dream home and driving your dream car. Visualize your desired bank balance and imagine your wallet filled with large bills or receiving large checks in the mail. Imagine your investments increasing in value. Continuously imagine money flowing to you and feel JOY and GRATITUDE for its arrival. (Later in the book we will be dedicating a whole chapter to the imagination. It is the real deal!). You can even imagine money coming in from known and unknown sources. Believe that million-dollar ideas are becoming available to you. When they come, embrace them and ACT upon them confidently. Learn how to invest your money and have it multiply while you sleep. Make space in your life for your desires to be fulfilled.

Never say out loud or think to yourself "I don't have this", "I will never have the money for that". You have to do the work to eliminate all negative thoughts from your vocabulary and in turn your mind. Negative thoughts create negative outcomes. Stop wasting your time attracting what you don't want. Continue to work with your new affirmations and abundance concepts until they are your new norm. Divine abundance in this world is overflowing beyond explanation! So set yourself up to receive…

and you can only do that if you change your thoughts. Feel that money floods in unstoppable! Get excited over this prospect of money pouring into your life like a strong endless tide!

Blocks to Wealth

Let's go back to the concept that money is energy, and you can either be open to this energy or block it. As we have touched upon, your negative thoughts will create a negative experience in your life, and any abundance of wealth will definitely disappear. What are some really specific things that you may be doing (and may not even know it!) that will be blocking wealth and abundance from being welcomed into your life?

Maybe you are in a rut. It happens to the best of us, no doubt! But how long you are in a rut is totally up to you. You always have the ability to make changes, but if you don't take action or ask questions about why (or ask for help) you will stay in this rut for a very long time. Maintaining a negative attitude and not taking responsibility for your life will be the death of your million-dollar dreams. I find that when people stay in ruts and are stagnant in their possible abundance, they usually tend to also be defensive about their failures. They are just soaking in negativity... Money is not going to want to get near any of that! Trust me!

Well, we couldn't have a complete discussion regarding what blocks abundance unless we mentioned jealousy, selfishness or being greedy. Again, these are extreme negative thoughts that can permeate your energy and block anything flowing to you. It is so important to learn how to shift your reactions and wish people well. For example, suppose you see someone with your dream car. It is expensive. It is beautiful. You wish it was yours!

Instead of getting jealous and upset about how this car is **not** YOURS, simply wish them well. I dare say, be happy for them. It may feel very counterintuitive at first, but this is a very important way of making that experience a positive one. If they can have a beautiful fancy car, then it can exist for you too. As you know by now, you have to keep your experiences and interactions positive so that you may allow things like your dream car to drive right into your life one day.

Even if someone has created their wealth through dishonesty or negative actions, not being critical or envious of their wealth is essential. Attainment of money by negative means will be dealt with by the Universe. These particular people may have lots of money but they also may lack happiness. I have come across many wealthy people that are paranoid of losing their money and experience constant fear that it will be taken from them. They begrudge their friends and family because they feel resentment that they are being taken advantage of since there's a silent expectation that they should readily share their wealth. They truly don't have peace in their life because they are always questioning the sincerity of all dealings with people. But still, don't judge. Stay positive and humble and allow the abundant energy to flow to you in a peaceful, unencumbered way.

Some people hold the notion that money is evil. If you are one of these people but still expect that you will be able to somehow sidestep this thought and attract money, you should know that it will likely never happen. And if you do attract it, it will likely be temporary. You can never attract something you feel negatively towards. So harboring this thought that "money is evil" is only constantly pushing it away. Really take a look at your feelings, and ensure this is not going on!

As you can see contradictions never work when it comes to working with your mindset. If you want to attract positivity, you have to think positively, especially when it comes to money.

- *I AM positive.*
- *I AM healthy.*
- *I AM wise.*
- *I AM prosperous.*
- *I AM mega money attractor.*
- *I AM generous.*

Allow Money to Flow In

Now that you understand all the ways you may be blocking abundance from flowing into your life, let's get to the good part: How to let it flow INTO your life! There are certain ways to actually attract money to you. It won't just show up unless you show up to your life in a particular way.

I love using one of my clients, Tena, as an example. When she had her first daughter, she was in the process of studying to be a life coach. She had a year off during her maternity leave from a salaried, non-inspiring job, and while looking after her baby, she organized the household and kept up her passionate life coach studies. Her income was lower due to her job leave, however, that year she was feeling magnificent. She had just become a mother which she was loving very much. She was also studying to fulfill a dream of being a life coach one day. This is important to note. She was working hard to build her skills as a life coach and fulfill her passion of helping people improve their lives. She was practicing what she was learning every day with everyone around her and adding joy into their lives! It was amazing to watch her attract abundance again and again that year! The money would miraculously flow in from places that could never be predicted. I feel this is a prime example of feeling joyous and attracting all that you desire effortlessly and easily. She received it happily and gratefully!

Once you've decided to adapt a positive mindset and established your goal of attracting wealth, open up to RECEIVE graciously. Since money is energy, there's an ample, infinite supply so feel free to ALLOW money to flow towards you. Always be thankful for this abundance that pours in, while having absolutely zero doubt that it will arrive. Ensure that you don't talk about lack and delete all contrary thoughts that question your ability to attract money. These negative thoughts are just an illusion. The truth is: You are an unstoppable money magnet!

Focusing on your wealth mindset will make all the difference! Here are some powerful affirmations to use:

- *I AM abundant.*
- *I love the vibration of money.*
- *Money floods into my life unstoppable!*
- *I love money and money loves me!*
- *I AM prosperous.*
- *I AM wealthy.*

When you visualize your dream life and claim it, you set the power of manifestation in motion. As I mentioned earlier, using the mantras throughout the day but especially first thing in the morning and last thing at night is very powerful. Those points in time allow these affirmation to sink into your subconscious mind and help ALTER the existing autopilot mindset you have going on. When you work on visualizing your dream life before you go to bed, you trigger your subconscious mind to work while you're sleeping. The subconscious mind then unites with the

For bonuses go to ...

Infinite mind to bring your desires into fruition. Again, another most important visualization tool that you must use is your imagination. You must picture yourself happily receiving the money you desire as if it has already occurred. You can visualize your bank balance increasing. You can visualize cash in your wallet. You can visualize receiving checks in the mail. Use your imagination in full color and engage all your senses! Always set this intention before you sleep, and believe that you have the power to attract wealth into your life. I have seen it happen in my life and in the lives of those around me. Trust the tools I share, and things will begin flowing to you! I'm excited to see what you will bring into your life!

I know that many of you reading this will be showing up to careers and jobs in hopes of advancing to places where you can be attracting even more money toward you. Many possibilities await. However, it is imperative that you use many of the aspects of a positive mindset that we have been talking about, which will help you achieve a business mindset. I have extensive experience in business and am excited to share with you what I know, and to help you get to the next level.

Chapter 7 Takeaways

- Your beliefs will bring riches into your life or create poverty.

- Money is an exchange of energy!

- The law of abundance states that in order to receive riches into your life, you must also be willing to give.

- The law of attraction functions with the power of love.

- Working on your wealth mindset (through visualization or using mantras) is a daily practice that is particularly potent first thing in the morning or before you go to bed.

- Your negativity will continuously block wealth from flowing into your life—don't go there! Stay positive!

Chapter 8

I AM SUCCESSFUL:
Creating a Life of Abundance
Through Your Work

> *"The secret of your success is*
> *determined by your daily agenda."*
> **– John C. Maxwell**

The purpose of your life is to be HAPPY! Think back to when you were a baby. Babies are inherently joyful and are ready to play and have fun. I am certain you smiled and giggled a lot; and when you got upset, you felt better pretty quickly. During infancy, our connection to Source (the Universe, God, however you frame it…) is exceptionally high. What happened as you grew into an adult? Where did that joy go? That immediate connection to Source? With each year that passes, you learn limiting beliefs that affect your life in every way. Your connection to Source weakens and your light continues to become more and more dim.

These limiting beliefs will show up in all aspects of your life and are deeply connected to how successful you feel or actually are today. The first thing you need to look at is what success means to you. What do you need in order to feel "successful" in your life? This is a very personal question as success can be defined in a myriad of ways. What you may see as success, your friends, family or colleagues may not. They may have their own definitions that you have to try to not be influenced by. At a certain point in your life, you may have been told what success is, but that is someone else's perspective. So, from this point on, what does it mean to you?

Is it being rewarded for your work and being recognized in a particular way? Is it making a certain amount of income per year?

For bonuses go to ...

What do you really desire? Start from there and see where your mind and heart take you. I can guess that when you begin sorting it out, you will feel that you haven't reached your full potential of what success is to you. And this is OK! That is why you are here. You are here to learn about what you can do to be overflowing with abundance. I want to examine the principles you must implement in order to be successful, no matter your vision. These steps will work for anyone, no matter how big their dream is. I want you to stand up and begin stepping out in your own unique way. As with everything we have been talking about, it all starts in your mind with your thoughts, and your powerful affirmations of course!

How to Be Successful

Some people in this world absolutely LOVE their work and what they do... and it shows! This may be a visual artist that paints exceptional landscapes, or a singer/songwriter that shares the most heart-warming songs. Or maybe it is a real estate broker that closes deals on multi-million-dollar properties, or a president of a company that leads their teams to exceptional growth. No matter what the path, I am sure you can agree that it is quite extraordinary to be in a position of doing what you love AND earning a handsome income doing it. I feel that is what success may look like for all of us. It certainly is for me! I not only want to always be loving what I am doing for work, but also to have the resources to have fun after work and do things, like have a great night out with my family or go on lovely vacations.

When you're passionate about your work, you will not only remain committed to your own growth, but you will shine and truly excel! It is essential that you have a clear vision for what you want to do, believe in yourself and take action. This is a tried-

and-true formula for manifesting not only a life you love, but also a life where you will truly be the best you can be and inspire others to do the same. Let's break it down step by step.

Are You Living Your Life Purpose?

This is a very important question to ask yourself. Sometimes we are programmed from infancy to follow a certain path delegated by our caregivers or by society. Examples of this is striving to enter the "right" college or university, and choosing a specific profession (like a doctor) because it is expected of you. Then one day, you wake up when you're in your mid 40s and realize that you are in the wrong job and are very miserable. This is often referred to as a mid-life crisis!

It is very important to have clarity on everything you wish to experience in your life. Happiness is derived from experience, not so much from material possessions. When you're at the end of life, you will likely remember the fun experiences you had and the people that mattered to you most, not your Rolex watch or Gucci bag. Therefore, it is important to write down all the experiences you wish to have and refresh this exercise on a regular basis.

Some of my experiences have been to travel to the Greek Islands, Italy and France. On my list are also experiences around health. I am very active and work out at the gym regularly. I also continue building my intellectual skills by researching various topics and studying areas of interest. You must be decisive. Indecisive people cannot be successful. Make a decision as soon as it comes up. Act right away when you feel the instinct to move forward. Avoid procrastination.

It is also important to have a plan. Only 5% of our population develops a plan. How will you fulfill your experiences? Write down (next to each experience) what you need to do to accomplish your goal as if anything and everything is possible. In other words, NOTHING is impossible. Don't worry about resources or money. Think outside the box! For example, when I traveled to Europe, I researched where I specifically wanted to visit and what the entire cost of the trip would be. Then I researched what the most affordable time of year would be for airfare cost, as well as weather. I ended up using some of my credit card points to pay for airfare and hotel costs, which really helped me save money. For my health goal, I decided on how many times per week I would go to the gym, what time of day and what type of routine I would engage in (cardio, weight training, etc.). For my intellectual goal, I chose specific books to read at night before going to bed, and certain YouTube channels to listen to while I was working out in the morning. This really helped me stay focused and execute all my goals. Be as specific as you can be, and affirm to fulfill all your desires, levering the law of attraction as discussed in this book.

Step #1: Identify What You Want to Manifest to Be Successful

Most people live their life stuck on repeat and maintaining the status quo. It is Groundhog Day over and over for several years. For many, it can feel very comfortable as usually this kind of life requires minimal effort. I'm sure this may sound very familiar because you may be experiencing this right now in your own life or can see someone close to you just going through the motions. In situations like this, usually what happens is that you reach old age and are filled with regret about not taking risks or creating new opportunities. You may feel like you were just dealt an unlucky hand of cards in your life.

Luck has nothing to do with anything! In your life, if you truly want something, you must possess a CRYSTAL-CLEAR vision of what you want and who you want to become. If you are not sure, there are two ways to hone in on it. First, you can think back to something that you saw someone have or be, and you felt that deep sense of longing inside, like you wish you had that something (be it a certain job, a loving relationship, project, etc.). Another way to identify this is to ASK the Universe for a little help in revealing your true passion in life. This can be very helpful, especially if you have spent years in the hamster wheel and really have not connected to things outside of your "day-to-day" in a long time. You may feel awkward, or you may not be sure how to achieve this. Ground yourself in positive energy and **feel** with confidence and delight that you will receive the information you need. Expect insight and clarity on the situation. When an inspiring opportunity shows up, make a decision to go for it! Successful people take action, while unsuccessful people make excuses.

When you have a clearer vision of what you want to manifest, get very SPECIFIC. The Universe cannot deliver what you want without extreme clarity. It is just not designed like that! A perfect example is ordering from a clothing online. If you wanted to order a jacket, you can't just order "a jacket." You have to choose everything from the style, size, color and pattern or fabric. You have to get specific, or you will literally be searching forever. This goes for your life as well. The more specific you are, the better!

In order to be successful, you need a clear VISION! If you are not sure what to do or what your next step might be, ASK the Universe to reveal your true passion in life. Stay open to what presents itself in your life that absolutely delights you. What are you passionate about? This is a big clue to explore that avenue.

When you are in this step of manifesting, stay positive and have high energy. Don't remain in a state of stress and anxiety, because that will not help the process but will only block it. If you take care of yourself in a positive manner, then the Universe will communicate to you all that you need to know. Ensure you are remaining in a high vibration by eating healthy, drinking plenty of water and avoiding alcohol or drugs.

- *I AM radiant.*
- *I AM magnetic.*
- *I AM beautiful.*
- *I AM optimistic.*
- *I AM adaptable.*

Step #2: Believe in Your Vision of Success

Once you have a clear vision of what you want, the second step is to BELIEVE that it's yours. CLAIM IT as yours and feel confident that you already own it. You may do this by actually imagining that your success has ALREADY been realized. Bring that vision into your mind's eye.

When you are in this stage of your manifestation process, commit to creating a very positive and nurturing environment for yourself. This will assist you in keeping a calm and positive mindset, which is imperative. This may look like listening to beautiful music that you love, or perhaps spending some time in nature. I can't emphasize enough about the power of nature. Clarity is imminent when you surround yourself in nature. Whether you're going for a peaceful nature walk or walking along a body of water, the insights you will receive when you empty your mind of irrelevant chatter are extraordinary. Treat yourself to a nice bath or massage or take the time to read a great book or watch a fun movie. Whatever you choose, ensure it is uplifting to your spirit, and stay clear from negative things like the news or social media. Try to limit time spent on social media. This will rob you of your peace of mind and precious time. Remember, you are guarding not only your energy now; you are also guarding your future potential to come through.

Of course, most of us will have to work our current jobs while we are manifesting our new ones. This is the way life is, and it is possible to do both! My friend Doris recently had this exact experience, and it was incredible to witness. She had a job that she wasn't necessarily excited about; however, she found deep gratitude for the work that helped pay her bills while she was continuing to expand her skills. She was also working on building new skills during her spare time for the future job she desired. She kept a positive mindset by finding things to appreciate in the moment, all the while keeping her eye on her future dream. She practiced her relentless visualization and gratitude every single day and did not give up. After only a few weeks, she was called into her manager's office—I bet you can guess what happened! She was referred to apply for a job that had come up, and it wasn't just any job. It was the dream job she had been working on manifesting (with a 25% salary increase, which was icing on the cake!). Upon starting her new role, she was greeted with appreciation for her expertise and fresh new ideas. Even at the onset, upper management had their eyes on her for future advancement opportunities. She was loving her new job and added so much value to the company.

It is so inspiring what can happen when you work with the power of appreciation and gratitude. Always be the best that you can be in your current job *while* you create your ideal job/business. And if you are connected to your passions or dream job now, then how about focusing on specialization? Make what you are working on specific so that you will be aligned with this very particular part of the market. And if you are working in an entry level job while you are still figuring this all out, do the best that you can each day. Always be willing to give more service than what you're being paid for. Be the exceptional employee that works longer hours to be more successful than everyone else that does their designated time. Employers recognize these exceptional employees and will reward them with higher income and greater career opportunities.

Discipline yourself to complete one task at a time. Concentrate and complete each task before moving to the next. Make a list of all your activities for the day. Leverage the 80/20 rule. Complete the 20% high impact activities first, which gets you 80% of your results. That is working smart! Manage your time wisely.

Strive to be the BEST you can possibly be within your profession! Find a mentor, hire a coach, sign up for a class and always be early, always be willing to take on more responsibilities... Do whatever you need to do in order to improve your skills. Stay focused on creating your best self, and trust that everything you want and need will come to you!

I AM *(fill this in with your greatest desire fulfilled)*.

Step #3: Take Action for Successful Results

This is the most crucial step when manifesting your life. You have determined exactly what you want. You are visualizing it and bettering yourself in order to be ready to receive it. And now it is time to take action toward it! You can't just sit there and hope that your success will magically arrive at your doorstep. You must be willing to walk toward it as well. This can also look like taking action when something is presented into your life and *feels* right.

For example, I had set a strong intention to go on a wellness retreat and came across one in France. After researching all the offerings, I resonated with this place and wanted to go. To my amazement after connecting with the founder of the company, he offered me a space at the retreat, all expenses paid! I accepted and trusted all the pieces would fall into place. My time off work was approved, my flights were booked without a hitch and the retreat went smoothly as I had visualized it to go. It really did feel as if everything was waiting for me to just say "yes" and take a step forward. I learned so much about myself and life while I was there. It is an experience I will always treasure.

When you feel an inspiring thought, take action immediately! Avoid tendencies of procrastination and take ownership of your goal. You must move forward, knowing that without a doubt success is yours! Sometimes the action you must take may show up as a big step. In this case, as I mentioned, you have to be willing to go with what *feels* right. The more connected you are to what you want and your visualizations, the easier it will be to take a major step. You may not know in your mind the outcome, but you will be able to feel in your heart and soul that this step is leading you to success. Sometimes the action you must take will be one small step every day. This is more self-directed and extremely important. It is essential that you schedule this time to work on small actions no matter what is going on in your life. Remember, you are doing this for your future self, and your future self will thank you!

- *I AM authentic.*
- *I AM genuine.*
- *I AM focused.*
- *I AM determined.*
- *I AM resilient.*

If you are willing to incorporate the above 3 steps, success can be yours. However, you must be committed to all of them. They don't work separately; they work in conjunction with each other. Personally, I like to think of it as a magic formula of sorts:

MENTAL POWER + PHYSICAL ACTION = SUCCESS

If you are ready and willing to commit to it, magic can and will happen in your life. I'm excited for you just thinking about it!

Create the Space: Train Your Mind to Think Positively

The mind is so paramount to the power of attracting an exceptional life that we mention this repeatedly throughout the book. When it comes down to it, the more you are able to hold positive thoughts in your mind, the more you are open to welcoming new and wonderful things into your life. Depending on where you are at, you may have to literally train your mind to shift from negative thoughts to more positive ones. While it may feel uncomfortable at times, this is absolutely necessary in order to allow the positive things to flow into your life. You will have to work in a constant cycle of recognizing a negative thought in your mind; and while being fully aware of the thought, do NOT fuel it with emotion. Just allow it to BE. Eventually, it will dissipate.

Suppressing negative feelings will only leave them to surface in many ways within your life experiences. The only way to remove this negativity is to release it. Negative feelings and emotions rise within our bodies because we may be triggered. Acknowledge the negative feeling, send it loving energy and recognize it simply as an old record player playing an outdated beat.

Get curious. Where is this negative feeling coming from? For example, I once had a negative feeling about a person that I felt had disappointed me. I kept thinking of this person repeatedly, and then I asked myself why. I realized that it wasn't about the person at all, and it was revealed to me that I had to value myself more. I had to forgive *myself* for putting too much energy into that relationship when I should have been prioritizing myself and my needs instead of allowing someone else to take my power. That was the truth behind the preoccupation. When I realized this, I forgave myself and the other person (energetically) and moved on. What an amazing opportunity to let go of a past lingering emotion and be free to move forward, skipping into the future with glee!

Give Back

An extremely important part of bringing success into your life is giving back. This means being of service to humanity and incorporating the sharing of wellness as part of your profession, no matter what it is. If you're selfish, then you will block the universal support that is always available to you.

A great way to give back in life is to volunteer or donate to a good cause. This can be done personally or even within the workplace. Over the years, I have participated in many charitable events as part of a sponsoring committee. It was always on my own personal time outside of work, but I really enjoyed these projects. I partnered with others who not only enjoyed it as well, but when we all came together, we did some incredible work! My most fond memory is being part of organizing a gala for a local hospital and raising $250,000 CAD. We had fun, the guests had fun and, all in all, it was an incredibly successful night. If you don't already regularly volunteer in some way, is there an organization or charity that you would love to work with? Or perhaps you'd like to organize your own fundraising efforts for something that means a lot to you. No matter the route you take, adding this aspect of giving back into your life will really keep the positive universal energy flowing your way and create even more support for your dreams to come to fruition. Great leaders will lead by always ensuring they are giving back.

The act of giving is almost like a secret "link" to manifestation. I had a friend that wanted to have and raise a child very badly. He and his spouse lined up a female donor and surrogate to carry the child. However, after many attempts, the pregnancy was unsuccessful. He discovered that, secretly, his spouse wasn't 100% on board with having a new baby. That negative energy was stifling and so powerful that it no doubt led to the surrogate never being able to have a successful term pregnancy. This is how POWERFUL the law of attraction is. It can bring your desires to you or refute them, just by your thoughts alone.

My friend didn't want to give up his dream, so I worked with him on course correcting the energy back to being positive and sending the clear message that a baby was welcome in their lives. I directed him to get involved with giving back specifically when it came to supporting children. He began visiting and donating money to a shelter in the neighborhood that specifically managed families and children. I coached him to stay positive and regularly work with affirmations such as, "I love my healthy baby" and "I AM so grateful to be a father." During the next time their surrogate was pregnant, he sent her warm and healing blessings. Of course, issues came up again, but this time my client remained positive, accepted support and trusted that everything would work out. I was so happy when their beautiful baby girl was born! She is exceptionally gifted with a photographic memory, and has brought enormous amounts of delight and joy into their lives and their home. Both parents are deeply in love with this magnificent child (even the spouse who initially was not on board).

What an incredible example of shifting the energy and attention to giving back to others in order to watch the Universe provide you with what you wish to manifest into your life. Always keep in mind that it isn't always about you, truly!

Ho'oponopono Method

The Ho'oponopono method is an excellent way to combat negative feelings and emotions forever! This is a Hawaiian practice of reconciliation and forgiveness. The Ho'oponopono method helps people heal deeply from their struggles to forgive themselves and others. This practice is thought to energetically move things back into balance and make them right. It is a powerful way to cleanse the body of guilt, shame, haunting memories, ill will or bad feelings that create a negative mindset.

Everything you experience happening is in your own mind. Everything you see and hear, and every person you meet, is your own unique experience. You may think it's "out there" and therefore absolves you of responsibility. However, because you're responsible for everything you think, that is not the case. This method is executed in steps, helping you accept responsibility for problems that are "out there" because they are in your mind and ultimately a part of you. When saying these statements, you take responsibility for something in your subconscious mind that has caused issues and conflict in your life.

For bonuses go to ...

The Four Basic Steps of Ho'oponopono

Each step creates miracles and has incredible power. Say each statement multiple times (out loud or in your head) but FEEL each emotion as you say it.

- *I'm sorry.* (Repentance)
- *Please forgive me.* (Forgiveness)
- *Thank you.* (Expressed gratitude)
- *I love you.* (Self-love)

In conjunction with the powerful method of Ho'oponopono, there are two very specific ways you can train your mind that may offer you some simple direction. The first is to start small in your visualization-to-manifestation process. Practicing it on a smaller scale will not only help you to train your mind, but it may also provide a source of inspiration when you can watch something come to fruition. Have fun and experiment with something! I always notice when I think of someone, they will contact me that day. It always delights me when that happens! I then know that my mind is in a clear and positive space. Or another example of this is when I will decide that I need to go in for a manicure right away. I am very clear and focused on my intention of getting an appointment that very day with my favorite manicurist (who is always booked!) and, lo and behold, there is always an appointment available for me.

The second way to stay connected to some positive mind training is to not allow yourself to get stuck in the past. In order to keep your mind clear and working on your manifestations, you must stop reflecting on what has not worked. LET IT GO NOW. It may not seem like a big deal; but trust me, it is paramount to bringing success into your life. Also, harboring any thoughts about the future is detrimental as well. In one of my leadership roles, I used to think that everything would be great when I had the right employees in place. It never worked. In your life, there will always be challenges to overcome and barriers to meet in the present. It is essential that you do that. Don't postpone your happiness! Implement your success now by staying in the present moment. This is the secret to success. Train your mind to stay alert and stay present. This is where the magic happens!

My client Christina is such a shining example of all I have been talking about. Christina desperately wanted to work from home so she could spend more time with her children. When we first met, she was commuting over two hours a day for work! She wanted to get that time back and add it to the time she could spend with her family. A pilot project was announced at her workplace, where they were offering people to keep their positions and work from home. She was thrilled! However, since demand was high, her employer was literally going to pull names from a hat to choose the team for the project. Christina kept talking about how she was "never going to get picked," and that is where I had to stop her in her tracks. Based on the manifestation process to bring success into her life, of course, she couldn't harbor thoughts like that! I advised her to start thinking about and visualizing her work-from-home situation. Which room in the house would be transformed into her home office? What would her new daily schedule look like? What time would she be able to spend with her kids that she didn't have right now? She gave this some thought and got excited visualizing her new day-to-day life that would be possible working from home. Christina put her name in the hat and made a strong CLAIM to realize this goal. She even cleared out the spare room where she decided she was going to work, and she set up a desk there. She refused to think anything counteractive to her desire, and guess what? Her name was chosen! She made it happen. Christina put the 3 steps to work and attracted this desire into her life.

For bonuses go to ...

Every new day is an opportunity for you to attract success into your life. Achieving success can be simple, fast and done with ease! When you doubt this process, you will encourage negative thoughts and struggle. But you can't get discouraged. Stay positive throughout your days no matter what you are faced with. Expect to be challenged. It will become easier the more determined you are to stay present, stay positive and maintain your successful goal with excitement. Remember: What you decide within your mind and your imagination, you will achieve through this space, time, dimensions and reality. Using the affirmations that I mentioned in the three steps will be a foundation you can then build your dreams upon.

- *I AM brilliant.*
- *I AM creator.*
- *I AM inspired.*
- *I AM courageous.*
- *I AM passionate*

When you change your mindset, you will begin to set the foundation for living in the highest vibrational frequencies possible. It is achievable and feels incredible.

What about business? Whether it be your career in the corporate world or as a self-employed entrepreneur, there are some business lessons that just stand the test of time and span across the business spectrum. I want to share some of these lessons with you so that you may harness your own personal power and be able to navigate business with ease and grace. Empowering yourself in these spaces will free up energy and time to continue to build your dreams.

Chapter 8 Takeaways:

- Your limiting beliefs are keeping you from realizing your most successful life.

- Understanding what you truly want and desire in your life is crucial and the first step to being open to bring it to you.

- The second step for success is claiming your vision with all your heart.

- Keeping your mind positive is the third necessary step to realize your ultimate vision for your life.

- Always remember this magic formula: *MENTAL POWER + PHYSICAL ACTION = SUCCESS*

- How positive you can stay in the face of adversity, is how well and effortlessly you will attract your vision.

Chapter 9

I AM A BUSINESS GURU:
Integrating Lessons from Business to Your Everyday Life

> *"Do what you do so well that they will want to see it again and bring their friends."*
> **– Walt Disney**

I've had over 25 years of experience in my career and want to share with you some major lessons I have learned—not only from a business perspective but also integrating your affirmations and ensuring you stay in a positive energetic state while you are open to the success flowing into your life. Business isn't just about climbing the corporate ladder or making the right decisions. It is also about keeping yourself open to possibilities and committing to your own progress.

Customer Service

Great customer service is a fundamental aspect of a successful business. When you are at your best, you will have satisfied customers. And that starts with exceptional customer service. I have the perfect example from my own career.

In my job at a major financial institution in Canada, I came across a client who is the CFO of a large global company. I was giving her advice on some strategies pertaining to the business. After our business discussion, I discovered that she was dealing with another financial institution in regard to her personal banking needs. I asked her if she would consider obtaining a second opinion, free of charge, through an advisor with my organization. I informed her that it was very prudent to ensure and confirm

For bonuses go to ...

that the plan that she had in place is indeed the correct plan that would help her achieve all her financial goals.

My objective was to let her know that I cared enough to ensure that her financial plan was sound. It was an opportunity to review the existing plan and, if it was on track, then that would affirm that her goals would be achieved. However, if we were able to provide added value, then we might potentially win her business. Either way, it was a win/win for my client. (This initiative on my part was purely advice driven. I was a salaried employee and would not be monetarily rewarded if she transferred her business to my organization). The answer she provided me was very interesting! She politely declined as she explained that she was extremely happy with her advisor. And when I asked her why, she indicated that she was not as well versed in the financial world and didn't understand how certain programs work (such as retirement planning) yet her advisor took the time and explained everything step by step to provide her with full clarity around the plan that was in place. This was a very helpful insight for me! Because the other adviser took the time to educate the client, it created loyalty and cemented the relationship.

Customer service is so important in business that I could literally write a whole book on the subject! It is the backbone of any business, no matter what it is, in getting ahead. It is why two businesses can be identical, but one will be more successful because of the exceptional customer service they provide. It is why customers can also be forgiving when things aren't perfect.

Great customer service will make people feel seen and taken care of. I once was a branch manager for a bank that had a rating system in place for all its branches. It was based solely on customer feedback and, essentially, if they would recommend our bank to their friends and family. At one point in time, my branch was under major renovations that weren't detectable from the outside; but of course, the inside was filled with dust and rearranged to accommodate the work happening. Surely one would think our service ratings would be low during such a time, but it was the opposite! We had one of the highest scores in the region! It was purely based on our excellent customer service. The employees were always smiling and upbeat, and they engaged clients about how excited they were for the renovations. It deflected from the mess and was engaging. The clients responded positively to our truly making the best out of what could otherwise be seen as a stressful situation. Customer service is all about **perception**.

From that year forward, we always had to up our game in order to stay on top. This is what happens when excellent service becomes the norm. Yes, it can be hard work to not just coast along and do an "okay" job. But it is worth it! This is what can take a business from just operating, to being truly successful and above the crowd. Excellence causes you to stand out.

If you want to improve your brand, it starts with increasing your client's satisfaction. The way to achieve this is by establishing an emotional connection with every client. Greet your clients as you would greet someone coming into your home. Make them feel comfortable and welcome. Perhaps even offer a beverage (if applicable) and encourage conversation. Take notes. Send a birthday card. Ask about family and their interests or business. Really get to know your clients, no matter how big of a business you manage or work for. You will immediately see this level of personalized customer service pay off. When treated personally and with great importance, clients will become very loyal and will also recommend you to their friends and family. Word of mouth is one of the best ways to reach people; it's an authentic way of gaining new clients.

Customer **feedback** is also essential. Asking your clients what they think is going well and what they think you can do to improve, is key to not only gaining more trust but to also providing direct insight into ways that you may continue to strengthen and grow your client base.

It's all about **connection.** Never lead with business in any interaction. Instead, lead with relationships. Start a genuine conversation about what is exciting in their life and even be willing to share something about your own life. We all want to be seen and heard, not just have things sold to us. Don't forget to use their name at least three times during your interaction (be sure to not overuse their name as it could get annoying for them).

Connection is the cornerstone of customer service and will only set you up for longevity and great success.

Communication Styles & Creating Relationships

It is so important to understand the various communication styles. I remember taking my first course in communication styles years ago and it forever changed how I approached customer service. It is essential to align your communication to reflect the other person's communication style. When you do this, you have a better chance of having the person "hear" you well and also making them feel that you hear them. When this is put into a context of a client relationship, they will easily feel seen and that you are authentically relating to them. Think back to my example of a client being happy with another advisor because they had laid everything out in a language that was more familiar to them. That is exactly what we are talking about here.

For example, I was speaking with a homemaker who was seeking advice on an education program for her children. She is not a banker, so I wasn't about to start throwing financial jargon at her! I approached the conversation using a language that was easier for her to understand and engage with. On the other hand, I have also dealt with clients that are extreme professionals, such as lawyers, CFOs and engineers, so I will match my communication tone to their more professional communication style.

If you need a starting place, begin by knowing the three styles of learning:

- Audio: what you hear
- Visual: what you see
- Kinesthetic: tactical or touch

The majority of people are visual learners (coupled with auditory or kinesthetic.) Because of this fact, I often use drawings or diagrams when explaining things to my clients. When I begin explaining something further by drawing or showing them a graph or chart, I can see the lightbulb go off in their head. They automatically become more engaged. This is what we are striving for. Can you think of a time where you just didn't understand something, but then someone explained it in another way, and it clicked? You automatically lean in, listen and are open to continue the conversation.

It takes practice, but as soon as you begin really treating each client as an individual that requires certain communication styles, you will notice a difference in your sales, numbers and overall customer retention. You will see greater success, feel more fulfilled and create more ease in your interactions.

Body Language

When talking to people or in group settings, it is important to be cognizant of your body language. The way you hold yourself will subconsciously send ideas and signals to others about who you are. So then, if you want to be empowered in someone's presence, it is important to know how you are coming across non-verbally to that person.

Maintain an open posture with your hands visible and palms facing upwards. Try to stay away from crossing your arms across your chest or clenching your fists. Ensure you make eye contact and nod your head when someone is speaking to confirm to them your engagement and understanding. They will then feel comfortable to continue speaking as you will be welcoming them without having to directly say anything.

Most importantly, practice active listening. Ask discovery questions to get a better understanding of the client's goals. Ask the client to prioritize their goals in order of importance. Restate and obtain agreement that you're on the same page. This is all done prior to communicating your recommendations. Always offer good advice as the client's Strategic Advisor. You want to establish a strong connection so that when a financial need comes up, the client will think of you and contact you directly.

Create a Financial Plan

When you were growing up, did you learn about personal finances and financial planning in school? No? Neither did I! I feel that our educational system is flawed because it doesn't teach practical courses around financial wellness. A part of your financial success is creating goals and then creating a plan to achieve them by leveraging I AM principles. Without a plan, you will not reach your goals, especially when it comes to financial ones. It's as simple as that!

There are many different types of goals that one may consider. Some goals include creating a Registered Retirement Savings Plan (RRSP), a Registered Education Savings Plan (RESP) for children, and Tax-Free Savings Accounts (TFSA) or Non-Registered Savings Programs. These are just a few investment strategies available to you when looking to save money in the long term. If you are looking to invest, there are many types of investment instruments, such as principle protected safe investments, savings accounts, stocks, bonds and mutual funds, which are taxed in various ways. Also, there are tax efficiency strategies that a good accountant can help you achieve and help you save a lot of money. I recommend taking some time and figuring out what you need for your future and what will work for you.

Also ensure you have an up-to-date Will and Powers of Attorney – one for your finances and the other for your health, all in place. This is a critical component of your life plan. If you have dependent children, this is even more important. In case something happens to you, your designated caregiver will be in charge of raising your children.

For bonuses go to ...

There is also the credit side of your financial plan. On the credit side, there are mortgages or home equity secured lines of credit for real estate purchases, unsecured lines of credit, different types of loans for major investments such as cars, business, etc., and, of course, credit cards. There are many tax-efficient strategies aligned to these products, and I recommend sitting down with a Financial Advisor/Planner at your financial institution and working with them to create a customized plan. (Here in Canada, many major banks offer this as a complimentary service. Why wouldn't you take advantage of that?)

When information is offered to us at lightning speed, at our fingertips, IGNORANCE is not an option! Educate yourself on what options are available to you. Take time to sit down with experts and get the help you need. Once you have identified your goals, only then can you leverage the power of I AM to attract your desires at lightning speed. Remember, that is the way things work in the Universe. You must be clear in your vision in order to attract what you need or desire toward you!

When I decided to buy a house, I completed a mortgage pre-qualifier to understand how much I was able to borrow from the bank. I also had some RRSPs saved up, which I used as part of my down payment along with our savings. I became very clear on how much I had to spend and created a budget. Shortly after this, I fell in love with a house we saw and wanted to purchase it, but it was a little over our budget. But something inside me said that I had to have this house. I clearly remember a moment during our tour when I was looking outside the kitchen window and I felt that I belonged there. This house not only checked all the boxes of what I wanted in a new home, but my family also fell in love with it. So, I went to work immediately to manifest the ownership of this house.

I leveraged the law of attraction to the fullest. I pictured myself in every area of the house feeling comfortable and as if it were already mine. In every waking moment, I felt excitement as I visualized myself inside the house, cooking in my beautiful kitchen, entertaining in various rooms and on the patio. I solidified this feeling of ownership within the core of my being. It was a gentle, playful feeling because I understand that the Universe acts quickly when there is no resistance. What I wanted and CLAIMED to be mine, was communicated to the Universe very clearly by the strong feelings of joy in my body. I let go with a sense of completion so that it would be. (I even told my mother that I had to have the house. She is a very spiritual and intuitive person, and she affirmed that I would!)

Within a few days, I put in my offer to purchase. There were multiple offers on the table, but I didn't lose hope or my focus on the fact that I wanted to own it. The owner, also a woman, informed them that she wanted to work with me. After several conversations, she dropped the price a little, which gave me the opportunity to purchase within my budget! I bought the house! It happened one week from the time I saw the house until we closed the deal, and I got possession one month later. Everything happened *quickly* and I was able to stay within my budget. This is how potent the law of attraction is!

I know that this can all feel like A LOT, especially if you aren't sure where to start or thinking about your finances is new to you. The very first step you can take is to make a list of all your financial goals and then reach out to experts (bankers, accountants, lawyers, real estate agents, mortgage specialists, financial advisors, etc.) to help you create a plan and execute it. Slowly but surely, you will start to see all the pieces of the bigger puzzle come together. At the end of the day, remember that the most important aspect of any plan is EXECUTION. Commit to staying the course!

How Does a Great Leader Operate?

You have innate spiritual gifts that you can choose to use for your success or not. This is often the sign of a great leader. Great leaders motivate their employees the way the employee wishes to be motivated. It might be praise, money, promotions, etc. They roll up their sleeves, if necessary, and work with their team to get the job done. They lead by example. They have a clear vision of the plan and are able to form strategies for successful implementation.

One of the skills you can leverage as a great leader is having the ability to see an upcoming project completed. Working backwards to foresee potential issues well in advance will certainly save a lot of time and energy. Great leaders apply common sense by thinking things through before executing on their strategy. They listen to their intuition and take action when it feels right to do so. They develop a sense of urgency by completing tasks quickly and efficiently. Leaders will collaborate with their teams to seek creative solutions for successful results.

Knowing how to apply the power of your mind, together with your powerful inner desire and positive feelings, you will achieve your desired results—without fail. Once you are committed to the goal, leveraging the power of I AM will work to align your request and make it a reality.

- *I AM a business guru.*
- *I AM successful.*
- *I AM completing my project on time.*

www.elenigiakatis.com

- *I AM leading a successful team.*
- *I AM attracting new business daily.*
- *I AM offering exceptional customer service.*
- *I AM creating a referral stream.*
- *I AM grateful.*

Use these affirmations multiple times throughout the day. As you know, with affirmations, if you say them with conviction and feel it in your body, your subconscious mind will claim it to be true. This can be the bridge to achieving great things in your life!

Lead with Kindness

When it comes down to it, the best way to establish and maintain great relationships with your clients and colleagues is to always meet them with kindness. No matter if the person upsets you or if they are getting upset, stay kind. Don't allow anyone to annoy you or just simply get upset as well. Stay in your power and realize that every opportunity you are faced with is an opportunity to learn and grow. It is an opportunity to learn about others and get curious. These are expansive moments and don't have to be ones of conflict. Always remember that in every difficulty, there lies a lesson. Learn from setbacks. This is wisdom!

Dare to have the courage to move forward to fulfill your greatest potential. When you decide to be fearless and persevere, you move toward success. If you're not afraid, you are not trying hard enough, and that will not help you move forward. Most people choose to stay still and feel safe. These individuals are the vast majority that work for leaders who execute their goals courageously. To become truly successful, you must *"do the thing you fear and the death of fear is certain"* (Mark Twain).

As a successful business guru, you should enjoy a bountiful life filled with joy, great health, money and all the luxuries you desire. Most importantly, you should feel positive, satisfied and peaceful. Once you master the ability to create, the world is your playground!

You must feel full of inspiration and excitement after diving into all these ways that you can empower yourself to live the life of your dreams. From your business life to your love life to your health and wellness, how it all leads to living life on a higher vibrational level is what you deserve! Let's wrap everything up and explore how you may leverage all this knowledge and truly be the pilot of your life.

Chapter 9 Takeaways:

- Exceptional customer service is a fundamental part of success in business.

- Always align your communication to reflect another's communication style.

- Part of your financial success is creating goals and then creating a plan to achieve them.

- Great leaders collaborate with their team and lead with kindness.

- When you commit to a goal, use "I AM successful" in order to stay aligned with positive feelings and desired results.

Chapter 10

I AM THE PILOT:
Getting Yourself Ready to Soar!

*"Keep moving forward. Stay the course. Remain focused.
Endure with power. You were born to win!"*
– **Beatrice Garrett**

We have come so far together! I am sure that you are feeling excited. Perhaps you may be feeling overwhelmed with all the new information that has been coming into your brain. But what about the new possibilities that are coming into your heart?

Let's take some time now to leverage all that you have learned and explore ways that you can stay the course. I'm hoping you have begun taking some time to establish some new and powerful routines that are naturally turning into opportunities where you are able to create your ideal life.

You are the pilot of your life! I want to review the tools you will take with you in order to stay the course. You are now creating deep change in your life. I never want you to revert back to the previous life you were leading—the old life where you felt stuck; the old life where you felt you had no say in the way things were going, where you felt disempowered and unhappy… You are leading a new EMPOWERED and beautiful life full of abundance and greatness!

Managing Change

Change is inevitable when you want to be more empowered in your life. However, most people just like to stick to the status quo and stay very, VERY comfortable. We love hanging out in our comfortable clothing, in our favorite comfortable chair, eating our favorite comfort foods... You can choose just to coast through life, and most of us do just that.

The other side of the coin is to get uncomfortable and welcome change into your life. The bottom line is that change involves work, but all the principles that have been outlined in this book will assist you to reach the next level of all aspects of your personal and professional life. But you must commit to practicing all the principles regularly. You can't expect yourself to change after doing your affirmations once, or because you have just decided that yes, you want to change. You will feel the push back from your mind and body. Remember that change is hard work. BUT on the other side of your effort, you have ease and abundance to look forward to. It just doesn't happen overnight.

Affirmation:

- *I AM accepting of change and welcome it.*
- *I AM capable of enjoying an incredible life filled with abundance, love, great health and laughter.*
- *I AM ready to level UP now.*

The Truth

I am sure you have heard the saying, "The truth shall set you free." But what does this actually mean in your life today? Think about when you were a baby. You lived in a joyful space most of the time. Of course, when you were hungry, in pain or uncomfortable for any reason, you would feel and express discontentment. Otherwise, you just lived in your joyful state and entertained yourself with anything and everything. But as you got older, you began learning more and more negative emotions from the people and environment around you.

You arrived on this planet living and breathing THE TRUTH. And that "truth" is that you were meant to live in happiness. This life that you are living is meant to be joyful. Having abundance and good health is the true state of the natural way of life. You can **choose** to live in this truth by connecting to your positive and loving emotions, or you can choose to stay in sorrow, ill health and poverty. Your life will look and feel so different if you choose negativity over positivity — the darkness over the light.

Because of the way society is set up, it requires a lot more EFFORT to think positively. No doubt! It is a choice to be positive and, depending on your life, certainly the trickier choice. To actually change your mind to think more positively, it takes a lot more willpower. When you feel uninspired or overwhelmed by things that are going on, remember that you are a powerful creator and can control the direction of your thoughts from negative to positive. When you feel defeated, remember to pause and take some time to slow down, breathe, meditate and regroup.

The truth is that there is ONE Universe that is based on love. There is an infinite well of positivity and abundance for you to tap into at any time through your thoughts alone. What you desire, you can bring into form with your thoughts. Release all fear and doubt from your mind and body… You can attract all that you desire! This is the TRUTH!

- *I AM exceptionally supported by the Universe.*
- *I know that everything will align perfectly in Divine time.*
- *I trust in the Universe's plan. The situation will work out for my highest good.*

For bonuses go to ...

- *I surrender and release all control. I allow the Universe to take charge!*
- *I AM fully supported, loved and nurtured.*

Your Ship Has Arrived

Many years ago, as I was just starting to build my skills as an advisor in the banking world, I remember feeling very frustrated at one point. I felt like I was at a standstill as I was working in a hybrid role and had mastered everything that was expected of me. My manager at the time told me to be patient. She kept saying, "Your ship will come in." I remember thinking, "What ship???... I'd rather fly! Surely a plane is faster..." But I took her advice and began practicing being calmer and more patient around it all. Just as I was really starting to lean into this new state of being, a hiring manager set up a meeting with me and offered me a new job that was in line with what I wanted to be doing next. This is how fast the Universe works!

This is about PATIENCE. When you are able to commit to clear, high standards for yourself in terms of your goals (and your life in general!), and combine that with a deep practice of patience, MAGIC happens. Impatience causes a huge barrier of resistance. You can think of it almost like an invisible shield that prevents you from attracting your desire. When you let go of the resistance and remain in a state of calm, the invisible shield disintegrates, and your desire can flow easily and unencumbered to you. You can practice patience anywhere proactively: in line at the grocery store, in traffic... anywhere! It doesn't always have to be when you are tested to do so. It can look like noticing when you are pushing for something to happen or wishing life would be quicker. Oftentimes, people give up just before a huge change is about to take place. They didn't realize that the gift they had been seeking was at the cusp of being delivered. They missed out. Patience is a virtue! Stay the course.

Adding in the practice of allowing life to flow will change the outcome of your desires. Things will happen more quickly and unexpectedly. You'll see!

- *I AM calm and peaceful.*
- *I AM giddy; I know that the Universe has a sense of humor.*
- *Therefore, I let go in a fun, playful way. I didn't sign up to be serious.*
- *I AM having fun, letting my hair down and enjoying the surprises that come along.*
- *I AM happy, healthy, intelligent and grateful!*

Maintaining a Positive Attitude

How do you maintain a positive attitude amongst everything that you have to manage in your life? One word: GRATITUDE. Gratitude has been touched upon a lot in this book, and for good reason. Gratitude brings you closer to the harmonious and creative power of the Universe. It prevents you from staying in a negative, uncooperative mindset. When you connect with gratitude, you open up a wealth of opportunities for creating and realizing your desires.

You know you need to revert to your gratitude practice when you feel uptight or upset, or you feel that something is unjust or when you feel someone has done you wrong. I often hear complaints from people about the levels of dissatisfaction that they are experiencing in their jobs. They constantly feel tired, overworked and unappreciated. They feel micromanaged and overwhelmed by all the demands that are placed upon them. They usually want to get up and quit! But of course, for most people, that is not an option. So, I encourage them to bring some gratitude practice even into thought spaces such as this. Perhaps you find yourself in a similar situation. Let's first start with feeling gratitude toward the paycheck that you are receiving from your employer. It may not only be supporting your everyday finances but also giving you opportunities to do things like taking a weekend away or going on a European vacation with someone you love. I challenge you to find at least a dozen more things that you are grateful for. It may start slow but soon the list will grow with ease.

Always be willing to manage your expectations around anything in your life. Never place anything too high on a pedestal. That way, you can keep yourself in a more grounded and neutral space and not set yourself up for disappointment. Disappointment always just leads you into a negative headspace. I stay away from expectations as much as I can. Of course, like anything, this too takes practice. See if you can take away your expectations for things and replace them with the power of gratitude (what you are already experiencing and grateful for.)

Your goal always is to first stay as close as possible to the harmonious, creative POWER of the Universe. The truth states that everything is already perfect. Your life, and everything in it, is as the Universe intended it to be. Everything that is opposing this vision is an illusion.

The Universe is on Your Side!

The Universe created our world as we know it in a positive, loving and enlightened manner. Over the years, negativity was introduced and has taken the reins. Look around you! Most people think of the worst-case scenario in most situations, instead of the best-case scenario. We have been conditioned to think negatively. Our thoughts are easily entwined in this negativity, so much so that we feel it in our bodies. Stress is one of the most popular emotions. People harness the negative state of stress and have a difficult time at pivoting from this negative emotion.

As indicated, the Universe created a PERFECT atmosphere of POSITIVITY. We, the human race, tamper with this. We created the illusion of negativity, struggle, lack, conflict, stress and other low vibrational emotions. The more we entertain this lack mindset, the more it grows and flourishes. You can water a poisonous plant or a vegetable plant. Both will grow tall and vibrant. The question is, which plant do you wish to consume?

Things are not always as they appear… Accepting appearances and taking to heart those suggestions is easy. To question everything and really decide what you feel is the TRUTH, is hard work and requires more diligent power. This is why so few people establish exceptional wealth and success. Most people will go with the flow and accept appearances as truth. They don't question the validity of these appearances and therefore remain small.

When we realize the fact that every thought has the potential to take form in the physical world, we will guard our focus on negative thoughts and accelerate positive thoughts that align to our goals. We would actually press the pedal to the metal and speed up these amazing thoughts into fruition!

When you BELIEVE this and accept it as TRUTH, watch your life powerfully TRANSFORM!

Affirm: ***I AM so happy and grateful that all my dreams are showing up into my physical reality.***

Creation 101

Another aspect of empowering yourself that is touched upon throughout the book, is creating a life that is aligned with your greatest desires and highest potential. You literally have the power to create your life from the inside out. You do NOT have to be a victim of your circumstances or anything negative that may be disrupting you.

As you pursue your desires, negative forces (such as your fearful thoughts or negative people) may be working to bring you down and prevent you from executing your goals. Have you stopped to think that your goals are possibly so magnificent that the dark forces will do everything in their power to diminish/eradicate your ability to achieve your goals? Perhaps what you want to introduce to the world is so profound that it will make an integral impact on humanity. You MUST have laser focus on the end result and not allow anything to enter your hemisphere that differs from this. You may even need to keep your goal private until you're ready to release it. Stay on guard of negative people that are committed to sabotaging your dreams. Be aware that negative forces are always at play and their prime focus is to keep everyone obedient and dreamless.

Become a fearless and powerful being that holds your dreams in high regard. You hold the power… Nobody can take this away from you! Nobody can control your thinking and, therefore, all your creative abilities can come to fruition because you think, feel and cultivate your personal dreams. Only YOU have this "I AM powerful" ability. Execute your free will.

Always hold a clear mental picture in your mind of what you desire. Perhaps you want to create a dream or vision board and place it somewhere you can refer to it often. You must stay focused and inspired! Think and feel positive emotions around your goals and visions at the two most critical times of day: first thing in the morning and last thing before you fall asleep. These are two of the many things that were mentioned throughout the book. And of course, use your affirmations, one of the most powerful tools of all!

Know your WHY. Then CLAIM it as yours. Through thick and thin, never stop believing it is yours. Let's say you want a high end watch. Take a photo of that specific watch and place it somewhere you will **see** it often. C**reate** space for it in somewhere in your room and always picture it sitting there ready for you to put it on your wrist. **Feel** the **excitement** of wearing the watch and checking the time. Decide this watch is yours in a fun manner and let it go. Allow it to be delivered to you. Don't worry about how/what/when/where. That is not your concern because it is already done. Affirm: *I am happy and grateful for my new watch and I love it!* *This* is just one small example of how to utilize the power of your mind to set yourself up to bring what you want into your life. You can apply this to anything!

Don't forget that it is also important to speak or think of what you desire as if it is already in your life. Have **FAITH** that it is already yours! It is here, NOW. This is very important. When you place what you want in the future, it will always be out of reach, and you will always be chasing it. Rather, when you put things in the present tense, you remove the energetic resistance around it and pave a way for its arrival.

Be willing to RECEIVE. Feel worthy of all the gifts the Universe wants to bring to you. Receive all the amazing things that come to you, wholeheartedly and with grace. Again, this will create a pathway for your desires to find you. When you feel a deep sense of self-worth, there is no stopping what you will be able to create in your life.

CLAIM it as yours. BELIEVE it is yours. Be willing to RECEIVE.

- *I AM attracting my every desire right now.*
- *I AM happy and grateful today.*

Training your mind can be compared to training your body. When you establish a weightlifting routine, you will start to notice positive results in your physical body. You will begin to notice your muscles becoming more toned, and your body may become trimmer. Remember this as you are working on everything in this book. Training your mind truly is an exercise in patience. You cannot obtain a positive mindset overnight! It takes daily practice. When you commit to a positive mindset, you will start to create all kinds of synchronicities in your life. You will begin noticing that many messages start popping up, and the possibility of manifesting your desires will begin happening very quickly if not instantly.

If you commit to executing all the advice given in this book, I know without a doubt that you will create a magnificent life enriched with joy, health, wealth, love and peace. You will live each day feeling healthy and amazing in your own skin. You will have financial freedom and incredible, loving and respectful relationships. You will go through each day feeling confident and worthy of all the good things that are coming to you. You will be a POWERFUL attractor of everything you desire.

Commit to not reverting back to who you were before. Practice every day and continue to pivot your life, flowing with happiness and abundance. You have the power to be part of the 5% of the world that has the most wealth, if that is what you desire. Anything can be yours if you continue to align yourself with the power of creating your future with excitement and positive energy. Whenever you slip, pick yourself back up and immediately continue forward. The most incredible life is waiting for you... Seize every present moment as you close the gap and leap into your positive and profound new life!

I AM EMPOWERED.

*"Life is an opportunity, benefit from it.
Life is beauty, admire it.
Life is a dream, realize it.
Life is a challenge, meet it.
Life is a duty, complete it.
Life is a game, play it.
Life is a promise, fulfill it.
Life is sorrow, overcome it.
Life is a song, sing it.
Life is a struggle, accept it.
Life is a tragedy, confront it.
Life is an adventure, dare it.
Life is luck, make it.
Life is too precious, do not destroy it.
Life is life, fight for it."*

– Mother Teresa

For bonuses go to ...

I truly wish that this book is helpful to you. It took me some time to complete as I was challenged with all kinds of obstacles that prevented me from sticking to my deadlines. My intent was always to write during a high vibrational state, and I had to use some of my own principles to complete this book.

If you need some help in mastering your mindset and overcoming some of your own personal issues, feel free to write to me!

I am available for coaching, mentorship and a broad range of speaking engagements.
Feel free to connect with me through any of my different channels...

I would love to hear from you!

I go by Eleni, but I'm also known as "Helen."

helengiakatis@gmail.com
Instagram: @alpha_powerful_
Facebook: Eleni Giakatis
Twitter: @HGiakatis
Tik Tok: @lenagiakat